D0305917

Capitalism is Dead: Peoplism Rules

Creating Success out of Corporate Chaos

Alec Reed

The McGraw·Hill Companies

London • Burr Ridge IL • New York • St Louis • San Francisco • Auckland
Bogotá • Caracas • Lisbon • Madrid • Mexico • Milan
Montreal • New Delhi • Panama • Paris • San Juan • São Paulo
Singapore • Sydney • Tokyo • Toronto

The *McGraw·Hill* Companies

Capitalism is Dead: Peoplism Rules
Creating Success out of Corporate Chaos
Alec Reed

0077103696

 **Professional**

Published by McGraw-Hill Professional
Shoppenhangers Road
Maidenhead
Berkshire
SL6 2QL
Telephone: 44 (0) 1628 502 500
Fax: 44 (0) 1628 770 224
Website: www.mcgraw.hill.co.uk

British Library Cataloguing in Publication Data
A catalogue record for this book is available from the British Library

Library of Congress Cataloguing in Publication Data
The Library of Congress data for this book is available from the Library
of Congress

Typeset by Gray Publishing, Tunbridge Wells, Kent
Text design by Robert Gray
Printed and bound in the UK by Clays Ltd, Bungay, Suffolk
Cover design by Fielding Design Ltd

McGraw-Hill books are available at special quantity discounts. Please
contact the Corporate Sales Executive at the above address.

Contents

Preface

'Peoplism' is a revolution. It is radically altering the formation and functioning of businesses and societies. I have been
researching and discussing this concept for many years now.
Building upon my belief that there are huge challenges
ahead, I set up a research programme into some of the
implications of peoplism in partnership with four leading
think-tanks: The Adam Smith Institute, Demos, The
Employment Policy Institute and The Smith Institute. These
think-tanks published their reports into specific areas of
concern – government, education, workplace dynamics and
business accounting – between 2000 and 2001.

While some may raise eyebrows at my assertion that capitalism is dead, the simple fact is that it no longer provides
sustainable competitive advantage. Capital is not the most
important factor of success. Practically anybody with a half-
decent business idea can find capital from somewhere;
getting the right people is a lot more difficult and a lot more
important. The success of my business has always been at the
mercy of my co-members, of which there are currently 2600.
Within the company we choose not to differentiate between
'employers' and 'employees', as the distinction seems dracon-
ian in an age where those who add value and drive success
cannot be so easily categorized.

Yet peoplism is not just a fancy term to describe the shift in
power in the workplace from capital to people. It describes a

movement that, alongside the considerable influence of globalization and technology, is fundamentally restructuring the wider society. Peoplism crowns a new rich and impoverishes a new poor, but it is no kinder than capitalism, and in fact it may make people more self-centred, and this worries me. New thinking and new solutions are urgently required.

The future is daunting, and I will not pretend that this book can provide all the answers. Many of the challenges identified and questions asked do not have simple solutions. An open mind and radical thinking are required on behalf of the reader.

I have a daily involvement in the public, private and charity sectors by virtue of my roles as Founder and Chairman of Reed Executive plc; Professor of Innovation and Enterprise at Royal Holloway, University of London; a City Academy sponsor; and Chairman of three charities: Ethiopiaid, Women at Risk and the Academy of Enterprise. This gives me the opportunity to identify trends in their infancy and appreciate the enormity of the changes and challenges posed by peoplism.

This book is the product of years of thinking and heated debate, and I am grateful to all those who have added thoughts and offered criticisms to my ideas.

Alec Reed

Acknowledgements

My first act must be to warmly thank McGraw-Hill for all their support during this project. In particular I would like to mention Elizabeth Choules, who, at the launch of my previous book, *Innovation in Human Resource Management*, first approached me with the idea of turning my long-held beliefs of the importance of peoplism into a published text. Elizabeth and her colleagues have continued to offer both support and sound advice throughout the duration of this project.

A special mention must also go to the very talented Louise Allanach who has worked with me as researcher on this book since its inception. The book would not have found its way to publication without all of her hard work and dedication, not to mention the help she gave me as first sounding board for, then synthesizer of, my original ideas. My thanks also to Michael Ward who joined the research team just as the writing process began in earnest and provided valuable input with regard to the peoplist business practices we uncovered in organizations around the UK and further afield. Other members of the Academy of Enterprise who helped on research tasks and proof-reading were Andrew Abernethy, Roger Bearn, Matt Hirst, Penny Hobman, Sarah Menzies-Gow, Janine Parry, Lyn Robinson, Ben Rutherford, Anna Sladen, Anna Taylor and Michael Whittaker.

Thanks must go to those business leaders who allowed us to interview them with a view to developing detailed case studies. The one defining characteristic common to all these organizations, different though they undoubtedly are, has been the openness of their leaders in discussing the particular responses to the peoplist revolution. One can only hope that we have captured the essence of peoplism alive in each of these organizations.

I also wish to extend my thanks to the foreword authors who gave generously of their time in contributing their thoughts to this project. The appraisals by Geoff Armstrong, George Cox, Michael Eysenck, Terence Kealey, Andrew Oswald, Madsen Pirie and Matthew Taylor serve to stimulate further debate around the key issues and themes in this book.

Foreword

**George Cox, Director General of
The Institute of Directors**

There is no doubt that we are in a world beset by huge change, almost everywhere we turn. In just half a century information technology (IT) has transformed both business and society, yet we still stand only on the brink of the IT revolution. Even those dramatic developments might be eclipsed by the forthcoming advances in biotechnology. Couple such developments with fundamental changes in society and demographics and the relentless advance of globalization, and we see a world in which mankind's activities have arguably outstripped his structures of government.

It is a world which is not only developing dramatically, but proving impossible to predict. With hindsight, today's situation and the overall direction in which it is leading will seem clear and logical. But from where we stand now it is impossible to see either clearly. We can detect the winds and currents of change but cannot be sure of our true position, nor our overall direction of progress nor our eventual destination.

Alec Reed's is a challenging book, all the more so because it is written by one of the UK's most successful entrepreneurs: a shaper of the business world, not just an observer. It brings together many of the major changes that we see happening and fits them into an overall cohesive framework.

Whether one agrees with his interpretation, it is difficult to argue with much of the underlying analysis. Certainly, a big change is taking place in the world of business and its underlying economics. If one doesn't agree with Alec Reed's views, then one has to ask what is the alternative picture of what is happening?

Andrew Oswald, Professor of Economics, Warwick University

Nope. Capitalism is not dead. But I do agree with much of the Reed thesis. 'Peoplism' is closer to ruling in 2002 than it was in 1952 or even 1982. And Peoplism, actually, is not a bad word for it.

The future will be dominated by extremes of human talent, to use my preferred language, and this is really what Alec Reed is talking about when he discusses Peoplism. So here I am on his side.

To an economist like me, the clearest evidence is found in statistics on the dispersion of wages. We know that inequality has risen quite remarkably in many western nations since the 1980s. The gap between the remuneration of the best people in a workplace and the worst people in a workplace has grown sharply. That can be seen starkly each Saturday on the soccer pitches of the major football clubs. The captain of Manchester United now makes about 500 times the earnings of the lowest quality footballer in professional British soccer. Yet in the 1950s, it was less than 50 times.

Much the same is found in boardrooms. The ratio of a chief executive's pay to a regular employee's pay is much larger than even 10 or 20 years ago.

Thus people, or to be precise your best people, are worth a lot more today. This is evidence of peoplism.

Why has wage inequality grown? In regular kinds of jobs, research suggests it is mainly because of new technology and partly a little because of growing international trade. In the extreme and most important jobs in society, what has happened is clear. It is that your best worker's 'marginal productivity' (i.e. their contribution to the firm) has gone up enormously. Think of David Beckham. When he curves a ball into the top of the goal, he can now be seen, on global television, by 100 million people or more. His counterpart in the 1950s was seen by a mere 30 000 spectators in the ground.

Audience and customer bases have exploded. Writ large, this kind of Beckham factor is everywhere. There, in a nutshell, is peoplism in action.

These pressures – the 'extreme return to talent' – will intensify throughout this century. We have to face up to them.

Geoff Armstrong, Chief Executive of the Chartered Institute of Personnel and Development

People and the way they are led, managed, developed and given the space to grow and contribute are at the heart of any successful enterprise.

Customers take for granted the physical features of whatever they buy. Quality, reliability, technical functionality, even price are not sustainable differentiators. Nor is investment in physical systems for manufacturing, distribution, information processing, or any of the traditional sources of competitive advantage. Nor, even, is a compliant workforce, loyally following orders from the top.

The critical tasks for any leader are to create a culture in which such enterprise can flourish and to build capacity through people that results in sustained, superior performance. Neither works in the absence of the other.

We have firm evidence linking positive business outcomes with progressive development and management of people. We know the components of high-performance working: teamworking, devolved decision making, continuous improvement and learning by doing, open and constructive communications, trust.

We know, too, how essential are leaders and managers who keep on raising their game, aiming higher up the value chain, creating cultures, values and relationships which elicit willing contribution, investing in people as the primary source of innovation not just as disposable human resources.

And we have the professional standards and body of knowledge on how to design and apply winning strategies through people. The challenge for organizations large and small is to make it happen, or they will be taken apart by competitors who do.

Michael W. Eysenck, Professor of Psychology, Royal Holloway University of London

Most outstanding ideas possess the characteristics of originality and indisputable rightness. In my opinion, Alec Reed's insight that modern societies are moving from the age of capitalism into the age of peoplism clearly satisfies both criteria for an outstanding idea. He is also right to argue that those companies claiming that their employees are their most valuable resource are often engaging in little more than hand waving, since in practice little is done to realize the potential possessed by their employees.

I am a psychologist with particular interests in individual differences and in occupational psychology. As a result, I completely agree with Alec Reed that it is vitally important for companies in the modern era to identify individuals with the ability to acquire knowledge and to use it effectively. That leads us on to the strangely neglected concept of 'intuitive intelligence'. In spite of the fact that most people recognize intuitive intelligence as a key ability of innovators and entrepreneurs, there is as yet a dearth of systematic research devoted to an understanding of exactly what is involved in high levels of intuitive intelligence. It is always useful when considering a relatively new concept to be able to think of concrete examples revealing its essence. In that connection, Alec Reed himself provides an excellent example of someone possessing an extremely high level of intuitive intelligence.

More generally, what we have in this book is a sketch map identifying many of the issues relating to peoplism which will need to be addressed systematically by the senior management of companies over the next several years. It will require the combined efforts of many experts (including psychologists) to fill in the details of this sketch map until a complete picture emerges. These efforts will undoubtedly be well rewarded, because it is very likely that those companies believing wholeheartedly in peoplism will prove markedly more successful in all ways than more traditional companies which do not. However, as they say, only time will tell.

Terence Kealey, Vice Chancellor of the University of Buckingham

In 1987 Professor Robert Solow of the Massachusetts Institute of Technology won the Nobel Prize in Economics for a paper he had published 30 years earlier under the title of 'Technical Change and the Aggregate Production Function'. Despite the inaccessible title, the paper is important because it showed that economic growth owes little to increases in physical capital (the then-conventional explanation) but much to increases in 'human capital' or, in Alec Reed's words, to 'peoplism'.

The details of Solow's paper are simple: he showed that American gross domestic product per capita doubled between 1909 and 1949, but that the nation's physical capital only rose by some 20 per cent. The difference, therefore, could only be accounted for by increases in human capital.

What is human capital? As Alec Reed explains in this book, human capital or peoplism is complex. Some of it is intellectual or scientific or technological: we increasingly know more, so we can invent ever better technologies to boost our wealth. The generation and transfer of knowledge, therefore, account for much economic growth, but that generation and transfer are peoplistic activities that need to be understood in peoplistic terms.

And much human capital is social. Here is a paradox: a cornerstone of economic growth is the contract, but the observance of a contract is irrational. This is because few contracts are simple exchanges. Most contracts are promissory: 'If you build an extension to my house, I will pay you on completion'. Strictly rational people, however, would not observe their promises, and they would cheat. But if everyone cheated, no commerce would be possible. Economies only thrive because most of us observe our contracts, however formally irrational that observance might be. Economic growth, therefore, is ultimately a matter of collective morality, which is rooted in peoplism.

More subtly, human capital or peoplism encompasses the myriad ways by which we co-operate – even as we compete – to our mutual advantage. The relationship between the individual as a selfish person and the individual as an altruistic one has occupied thinkers for millennia from fields as diverse as theology, philosophy, politics, economics, psychology, sociology and evolutionary biology. In this remarkable book, Alec Reed makes his own cross-disciplinary contribution to one of humanity's oldest issues, the issue of peoplism.

Matthew Taylor, Director, IPPR

There is little that is inevitable about the future. As we in the rich world move from a consciousness shaped by tradition and deference, social homogeneity and economic shortage there is the possibility of a new world of self-government, integrated diversity, the pursuit of quality of life. But there are also the risks of cynicism, separatism and hedonism. Alec Reed reminds all of us that we must choose to create the future that we want. And he is right that the central challenge is how we respond to the ever-growing importance of intelligence and creativity in determining the success of individuals, organizations and societies. Too often reform in the public private and voluntary sectors is about modernizing the old ways rather than the transformation that is surely necessary. The core task for progressives is to create a new form of collectivism based not on the old cleavages and loyalties but on the conscious desire of modern people to build better organizations and societies. Alec Reed's provocative book helps us to ask the right questions and begins to sketch out some of the new ways of thinking we will need if we are to exploit the immense opportunities now at our fingertips.

Dr Madsen Pirie, President, The Adam Smith Institute

The ancient Greek philosophers divided themselves between supporters of Parmenides, who thought everything stayed the same despite surface appearances, and those of Heraclitus, who thought that everything was in perpetual change. There is no doubt that in the modern economy, it is Heraclitus who rules. We find ourselves in a river with new waters flowing ever about us.

One of the major factors which accelerates that change is the transition, identified by Alec Reed, from an economy based on capital to one based on people. Wealth is no longer created on a base of fixed capital, but increasingly on the talents and abilities of individuals. It is gifted people with marketable skills who drive the modern economy. Because people are more mobile than fixed plant and machinery, the economy itself changes more rapidly.

This transition has far-reaching consequences, not only for businesses involved in the wealth-creating process, but for the individuals themselves, those whose abilities are now the prime assets of those corporations. There are consequences, too, for governments, nations and societies. Only those institutions which are flexible enough to adapt to the new circumstances can benefit from these changes.

Talent and skill are the new precious metals which denote wealth in the modern world. They have to be encouraged, developed, attracted and retained. Companies and countries which do this successfully can survive and prosper; the others cannot. The units of a capital economy did not have minds of their own. They could be deployed by those who owned and managed them. People, however, are autonomous. They have purposive minds. They can move at will. They cannot be ordered about, as capital can. They have to be enticed and rewarded.

What Alec Reed has identified is not just a change in economic process. It is a fundamental shift in power away from organizations and toward individuals. It is a change which will do more than any other to colour and shape the world of the future.

Introduction

The changing economies

Agricultural economy	Industrial economy	Creative economy
Feudalism	**Capitalism**	**Peoplism**
150 BC	AD 1900	AD 1990

It was around 150 BC when the agricultural revolution began to unfold, transforming society with the invention of the plough and making large-scale agricultural production possible. Land defined status and was by far the most important economic factor of production. Labour was low skilled, low paid and easily replaced. In pre-industrial society the labour force was engaged overwhelmingly in the extractive industries of fishing, forestry and agriculture.

The industrial revolution arrived 18 centuries later, in the 1760s. Large factories were erected on small pieces of land. In the industrial economy, capital became the most important economic factor, while labour was minimally trained, semi-skilled, low paid and of limited importance. In place of the peasant farmer came the factory worker. Industrial energy replaced raw muscle as the provider of power and productivity, developing the art of making more with less. The workplace was organized on the basis of functional tasks, not people-based roles.

Two and a half centuries later we are entering the peoplist revolution. In our creative economy land and capital are of limited importance, their ease of accessibility negating any competitive advantage they may offer. The most important driver of value creation is the enterprise and creativity of individuals, qualities that only they themselves can own. *Peoplism* defines the overwhelming importance of (some) people in modern society. Peoplism has succeeded capitalism. The implications for nations and individuals are considerable, and shall be examined throughout this book. It is in the sphere of business that some of the most fundamental changes are occurring. The aim of this book is also to highlight the most pressing challenges in the business world, and to offer solutions.

Business implications of peoplism

Although companies have been confidently declaring that people are their most important asset for some years now (a ludicrous assertion; how can a company *own* a person?), the real consequences of such statements are yet to bite. Indeed, while such rhetoric is espoused by all of the FTSE 100 CEOs and chairpeople in corporate literature, the reality is that of those 100 companies, only 20 per cent have supported their commitment to people as their 'most important asset' by appointing a Human Resources Director to their executive board. Yet you can be sure that all have a finance director on their board. This rhetoric–reality gap cannot continue for much longer. The people economy is upon us. We are set to witness fundamental and cataclysmic changes to the way we conduct business in the near future. Hold on tight!

Let us not forget that it was 20–30 years after the onset of the industrial revolution before the significant changes to society occurred. The evolutions of travel, industry and communication came decades after the invention of the railways as society adapted to its new environment. Similarly, electricity was discovered long before it gained industrial application, and although the initial uptake was slow, it later accelerated in use to massive effect throughout the economy. The first commercial power stations were built in the 1880s, but less than 1 per cent of all power used by companies in the USA in 1890 was generated by electricity, with steam or water remaining preferred sources. In 1900, that figure had risen to 5 per cent and by 1930 to 76 per cent. By that time, electricity had transformed the industrial economy, in the way that the internet revolution and innovation are now transforming the people economy. A similar, but faster, pattern of exponential growth and diversity of application should be expected.

The death of capitalism

In the capitalist economy the factors of production – land, labour and capital – were combined in the pursuit of producing goods and services to be sold to consumers. It was the function of enterprising individuals to chase the capital they required for their proposed commercial activity, with the obvious consequence that those who held the capital were in the driving seat. Banks and the banking system were at the cornerstone of the capitalist system as the central depository of the system's most important resource.

The end of capitalism and onset of peoplism can be seen as a natural progression in the development of our consumer-driven society. Capitalism served society's consumption needs up until a point. 'Fordism', a management approach typical of capitalism in the early to mid-twentieth century, produced uniform products for consumers who placed little value on diversity, and permitted an overwhelming management focus on maximizing resource utilization. Capitalism was successful in raising individuals' living standards, and fuelled a consumer-driven society. The effect of this was to place new competences at the heart of value creation, with innovation replacing standardization, and creativity replacing control.

The infrastructure that supported capitalism remains in place. Accounting, having moved away from its tradition of conservatism, has flirted with creativity and got burnt. Equity markets have suffered from the failure to construct a method of pricing enterprises that offer any longevity of value in a just manner, and are prone to bubbles which inevitably burst.

The fallout from Enron, Worldcom and Tyco was as much the result of inherently disconnected practice within the banking as the accounting sector, and several banks have been found wanting over the last 3–4 years. They are under increasing pressure to provide seemingly ever-increasing returns on their capital reserves. This pressure has created a culture of risky investments hidden within a matrix of complicated holdings, cross-holdings, liabilities and exposures. The corporate banking sector has been found guilty of propping up failing enterprises.

Banks have turned the wrong way in their strategies for coping with a changed set of circumstances. They have continued to expand their activities as 'capital' experts offering different investment/banking activities without having developed their ability to identify the new areas into which this capital should flow.

Capitalist institutions need to go through a new process of *'Idea-lization'*, a process as significant as the industrialization that came before it. Idea-lization starts first with a recognition that the very fundamentals of wealth generation have shifted, and the relationship between capital and enterprise has fundamentally altered in favour of the latter. This relationship remains in flux. Banks, investment houses and venture capitalists have been badly burnt by the dotcom frenzy. The reason for this was that while capital rich, they failed to understand the basis of the new relationship that capital is obliged to have with enterprising individuals. The new depositories of economies' most important resources have become individuals and collections of individuals.

Of course, the importance of capital as a factor of production has not evaporated. Capital is still important, just as land still had a role to play when capitalism subsumed feudalism as the economic age of the time. However, capital is not as important as human talent and ability. After all, a talented individual can make a good living working in a coffee shop with a laptop and a mobile phone. In addition, capital no longer provides competitive advantage because it is now so widely available. The more a resource is accessible to competitors, the less competitive advantage it confers. There can be little doubt about what does confer competitive advantage. Some people do. Capitalism is Dead: Peoplism Rules.

Peoplism is an economic revolution. Like economic revolutions before, the political and social consequences of this movement will be extensive. In no arena is this more acute or more important than in business. *Capitalism is Dead: Peoplism Rules* begins with a snapshot of the people economy in 2002. Chapter 1 provides a detailed view of the 'naked individual', while Chapter 2 narrows its sights on the business implications of the naked individual. It looks at the changing relationship between employers and employees, and outlines some of the most corrosive examples of disconnected thinking which are acting against the interests of companies, and indeed countries. Chapter 3 explores the internal business consequences of peoplism, specifically in regard to organizational structures and branding. Life cycles for both inputs (materials and employees) and outputs (products and services) are shortening in every industry as the notion of 'a job for life' fades into workplace folklore and continual innovation drives the economy. External considerations such as the race to prove corporate social responsibility and the need to avoid the arrogance of success are detailed in Chapter 4. The next three chapters examine the implications for human resource management, accountancy and communications in turn, signposting the radical redirection each function must take and detailing how best to do so. The book closes with a glimpse into the daunting future.

Globalization and information technology have resulted in an oversupply of almost all goods and services, leading to the commoditization of just about everything. With many goods and services, price is the only choice factor. Where price is the main determinant of the market, profit margins are inevitably driven down. The only way, therefore, that profit can be maintained is through innovation. And the only way that companies can be innovative is through their people: creative people.

The aim of this book is to highlight the immense challenges facing companies attempting to readjust their structure and functioning in the people economy. The five key challenges are:

- to refocus human resource management

- to realign accounting practice with the key value drivers

- to reposition marketing where it is off-target

- to ensure that organizational structures are not stifling success

- to allow corporate culture to evolve.

What follows is a brief snapshot of the people economy 2002, illustrating the myriad conflicting consequences and effects of the peoplist revolution. Many of the consequences are extremely positive, ushering in the best of times for the individuals, corporations and nation-states most able to take advantage. The worst of times looms over a similarly eclectic selection of demographic and social groups. The premium on human talent is the essence of peoplism, yet there exists impotence in society as a result of foolish thinking at many levels. Peoplism ushers in a new distinction between the 'haves' and the 'have nots', replacing the growing irrelevance of inherited wealth with individuals who have the skills to thrive in the people economy and those who do not.

The people economy: snapshot, 2002

It is the best of times ...

Real incomes have doubled during the past 25 years, and are set do so again in the next 25. Standards of living are increasing for a significant portion of the global population and individuals are reaping the reward for their talents, with 'skillionnaires' (those individuals who have *made* their millions of dollars or euros as opposed to inheriting them) reigning supreme in the leagues of the most wealthy. Citizens wield ever-greater political and economic power, and those blessed with an entrepreneurial spirit are no longer blighted by failure in an era in which talent and ambition furnish recurrent opportunity. Global economic growth is accelerating and the World Bank estimates that global poverty will be halved by 2015.[1]

It is the worst of times ...

Traditional relationships of succour and security such as the family, the Church and the community are dissolving. Inequalities in wealth, and in the opportunities to create wealth, still exist domestically and globally. The age-old problem of refugees and asylum seekers persists, together with an increasing rush of economic exiles as individuals go to desperate lengths to realize the attractive economic opportunities of the people economy. The power and influence of nation-states are being eroded. Western welfare states do not have the resources to struggle on much longer in a globalized world and corporations are increasingly stepping in to take up the slack for their chosen few. There is a silver lining, and Chapter 1 demonstrates where to find it. Globalization and advanced technologies have not, yet, brought increased wealth and prosperity to all states. No fewer than 80 countries have a lower income, measured on a per capita basis, than in the early 1990s. Three billion citizens, representing over 45 per cent of the world's population, are living on less than US$2 a day, with over one-fifth (1.2 billion) living on less than $1. In many aspects of society, government is struggling to maintain control and state management has gone to extraordinary lengths as a result, with a record number of adults and children being retained in British prisons.[2]

It is the age of wisdom ...

Although knowledge is incredibly important in the people economy, it is not as important as the ability of an individual to *use* their knowledge. Intelligence is key, but *intuitive* intelligence is the real goal for employers seeking to win the war for talent, and strategies to test for and measure it are set out in Chapter 5. Empowerment of talent is real. Individuals whose skills are in high demand and for whom a change of employer is always an option are exercising increasing control over the wealth they create, and who they create it for.

In some parts of the world, wisdom and ability trump nationality. Sven Goran Eriksson is the thin end of the wedge, and after his success in running the English football team, it is only a matter of time before someone of the calibre of Bill Clinton is wooed in to run another country. Those with the skills to succeed will thrive regardless of their country of domicile, eliminating the ties of ethnicity and eroding national borders.

It is the age of foolishness ...

Inflated payoffs and golden goodbyes are being ever swollen to provide soft landings for non-achievers. We live in a culture of rewarding failures and, as Chapter 4 outlines, it is imperative to avoid the arrogance of success. Extravagant golden handshakes and golden handcuffs are prolific on the talent battlegrounds. The problems are not just in the sphere of business. Many charities will discover that they are facing the wrong way; their strategic aims no longer help those who are most in need. The winners and losers of the people economy are different to those of the capitalist economy. Organizations that offer money to the blind, the disabled and the socially excluded will find themselves redundant as the creative and innovative members of these groups thrive under a new order where intellectual creativity dwarfs physical capability.

It is the epoch of belief ...

The people economy is not just about performance; it succeeds or fails at the level of intuitions and instincts. The world changes as a consequence of our expectations and beliefs. The acute ebbing and flowing of the Nasdaq during the dotcom boom was less about the physical capabilities of the technology than the belief of the investors in that technology. Technology is growing in flea-years, and intuition and instinct are elemental for business success as information and spin swamp decision takers. In the USA, 75 per cent of boys believe they will be earning a million-dollar salary by the time they reach their 40th birthday.[3] People believe that national borders are no longer sacrosanct, and thus to many intents and purposes they do not exist. The spread and speed of information are rendering legal and geographical jurisdictions defunct and making management communication strategies, which are outlined in Chapter 7, key value drivers for the future.

It is the epoch of incredulity ...

Much incredulity comes from the bewildering pace of change. Of all the scientists who ever lived, more than 90 per cent are alive today. The stock of scientific knowledge is currently doubling every 5–7 years; by 2020 it will double every 73 days. In 2010 the number of IT graduates in India will be greater than the entire population of the UK. The future is as daunting, making Chapter 9 a must read.

The new playing field rolled out in the people economy is a cause for concern, but more importantly it is an opportunity for employers and employees. Business leaders must be alert to these developments and generate responsive strategies so that their companies can best cope. It is up to them to guide their organizations through the early fallout from the seismic changes that peoplism has induced.

This is the people economy. It *is* the best of times. It *is* the worst of times. It *is* the age of wisdom, and the age of foolishness. It *is* the epoch of belief, and the epoch of incredulity. We have everything before us. (With apologies to Charles Dickens, *A Tale of Two Cities*.)

As the text introduces terms that may be new to the reader, they are defined in a glossary at the end of the book. To further assist the reader, their first occurrence in the text is identified by highlighting them in bold italics.

CHAPTER I

The naked individual

Peoplism strips individuals bare of much of the protective padding of the past as many traditional support structures, including the family and the community, lose the relevance they once held. There is a distinctive split between the *peoplist* rich, those with *enterprise skills* such as creativity, innovation, the ability to solve problems and create opportunities, and the peoplist poor, those without such skills. Serious challenges lie ahead for governments, employers and charities in accommodating naked individuals.

The emergence of the naked individual brings significant challenges for business. *Co-members* and business leaders are naked individuals, and companies must be responsive to the new challenges they face.

Peoplist rich: capitalist poor

That the advent of the people economy marks a time of social polarization between states has been established. It is also a time of massive disparities in wealth *within* states. The net worth of the top 1 per cent of Americans is greater than that of the bottom 95 per cent. In 2001 there were 250 billionaires in the USA, compared with 82 in 1999. Individual wealth has reached unprecedented levels; the three richest people in the world, Bill Gates, Warren Buffett and Paul Allen, have total assets greater than the combined gross national product (GNP) of the 43 least developed countries. Britain boasts more than 68 500 millionaires.[4] Since the early 1990s, the sum required to win one of the top 200 places in the *Sunday Times* Annual Rich List has tripled from £50 million to £150 million. The number of people in the UK earning over £100 000 a year has increased by 50 per cent in 4 years, to over 350 000.

Homeowners are the new rich, and houses are the new pension schemes. Average house prices have grown 100-fold since 1945, 10-fold since 1973 and 2-fold since 1988.[5] A garage in Kensington, London, can now cost £150 000.

Sportspeople, and particularly footballers, are reaping the benefits of being talented individuals in a classic example of *peoplism*. English football is the richest league in the world and the first to break through the billion pound barrier. However, the majority of clubs made a loss in 2000 by attempting to keep up with the spiralling wage demands of their key personnel. Research by Deloitte and Touche revealed that in the 1999–2000 football season, just 10 premier league clubs (out of 20) and 5 football league clubs (out of 72) made an operating profit. The report made a link to the 21 per cent increase in wage costs over the same period. Seven out of every ten clubs had a wage bill in excess of 70 per cent of their income, and 16 league clubs, including Blackburn Rovers and Brentford, had wage bills exceeding

100 per cent of their turnover. In 2002, a 24 per cent lift in payroll costs to over £30 million left Aston Villa with a pre-tax loss of £350 000. It is the players and managers who are the stars, and the capitalist infrastructure is helpless to prevent the high wage demands of the real creators of value. While the wage demands will eventually self-regulate, there is a significant way to go before any levelling off of the upward trend will be seen, as those with talent continue to push for increased rewards.

Off the pitch, the real winners in the people economy are those with the talent, creativity and innovation so desperately needed to succeed in business, and similar issues of increased remuneration, retention problems and talent management will increasingly affect companies of all sizes.

Peoplism represents the decisive supersession of talent and brains over brawn. Yet intelligence is of little worth if it cannot be channelled for a purpose. Knowledge per se holds no competitive advantage, for it is only a product of memory and learning; and the internet makes all information instantly accessible. The aim for individuals, and the goal for employers, is to be '*intuitively intelligent*'. The new rich therefore do not necessarily have knowledge, but they certainly have *nous*. In this world, winners take all, but losers have few places to hide. Many organizations offer opportunities, but few now offer protection, as can be seen from an increasing number of companies adopting Jack Welch quota-style sackings of those unable or unwilling to make the grade. To see if such an approach suits your business, turn to Chapter 5.

Individuals disengaged from the state

The traditional powers that states once wielded over the wealth of their citizens, and the ability of governments to protect their weakest citizens, are waning. Peoplism erodes the powers of states, and makes many traditional state functions impossible to perform.

Globalization restricts the ability of governments to levy taxes on exports, as more countries compete in the global market for inward investment. Soon, all but the smallest companies will be located where profit can be maximized and regulation is minimized. Peoplism dictates that the most sought-after intellectual resources will often go with them, particularly if their government of domicile should adopt objectionable taxes on income in order to finance a welfare system, or impose strict regulations on working hours. A prime example of a trend gathering pace is the European hauliers who are able to tax their heavy goods vehicles at a more favourable rate on the European continent, and then work in the UK using their tax advantage to undercut British prices. This is the modern-day economic equivalent of maritime 'flags of convenience'. The internet provider Freeserve is preparing to sue the British Government over a tax dispute it claims favours foreign competitors. Freeserve is concerned that AOL Time Warner is exempt from charging its British customers value-added tax (VAT) because it is based outside the European Union (EU), and the company has threatened to move its head office overseas if the tax discrepancy is not removed. In the same way that unfavourable domestic rules on gambling were scrapped after a plethora of international competitors became happy to offer better deals, our global economy will not tolerate fragmented parochial tax systems. The desire and capability of organizations and individuals to choose the country in which they are based for optimal financial benefit is crippling the ability of governments to use taxation for financing social welfare measures. American companies that paid less than zero federal income taxes in 1998, because of rebates, included Texaco, Chevron, PepsiCo, Enron and General Motors.

The semblance that the state is able to cater for the diversity of choice demanded for services is already being stretched thin. It will soon snap. The UK health service accidentally kills 20 000 people a year. One hundred National Health Service (NHS) patients lose their sight each week because they fail to get treatment quickly enough.[6] One-fifth of all Britons leave school unable to read.[7] The third world reaches everywhere. Even the world's richest nations are home to more than 100 million people who live below the poverty line.[8] In the 'rich' Western world, at least 37 million people are unemployed, 10 million people are homeless and nearly 200 million have a life expectancy of less than 60 years. Over 16 per cent of Americans live in poverty despite the fact their homeland is the richest on Earth. One-quarter of American children live in poverty.[9] The number of British adults in completely non-working households increased to more than four million in 2001, increasing fears of growth in child poverty.[10] Governments are becoming severely restricted in the actions they are able to take, and the strict separation of state obligations and business responsibilities is becoming increasingly blurred. Peoplists best able to exploit the opportunities and advantages open to them will simply not subsidize such incompetence.

The uniformity of approach to the delivery of public services, with attention to a restricted pool of service providers, is inadequate. In the UK, ministers are already using the private sector to give patients more choice about where they are treated, with more than 230 operational public–private partnerships and 450 more ready to roll.[11] Part of the state management involves farming-out patients for quicker treatment abroad. The UK Government is already reacting to a decision by a supranational body, the European Court, which ruled in July 2001 that patients have the right to be referred elsewhere in the EU if unable to receive treatment without 'undue delay' in their home country. How long before this goes outside EU borders? State management involves hitting targets by any means.

In the national politics of the vast majority of developed countries, leadership has been replaced by good management. Capable individuals neither need nor desire others to provide for them, or to make decisions about their financial well-being on their behalf. In the same way that the creative economy cannot be driven by traditional command and control management techniques (and can only truly prosper under delegation and trust), the centralized ruling structures of the past are no longer suitable, and a devolved form of state management is required. As peoplism erodes the activities of states, companies will increasingly step into the breach of service provision for their talented workers. The responsibilities between the entities will merge and overlap, giving birth to the peoplist 'corpora-state'.

The power of public opinion has gained much strength in recent years. Government is executed by focus groups and the press. The UK Government was the biggest spender on advertising in 2001. Spending soared by 39 per cent to over £140 million, more than that spent by Procter & Gamble and BT, in second and third place.[12] There exists a marked contradiction: voter apathy has reached unprecedented levels, in spite of – or perhaps because of – increasingly frenetic attempts by politicians to woo the sceptics. There is a mood of corrosive cynicism.

This disengagement between state and citizen is destructive, as evidenced by an ICM poll in 2001 which revealed that 12 per cent of adults would not report a murder to the police, and 70 per cent would not report a brawl. For every crime that is reported, at least four are not.[13] Of those eligible to vote in 2001, 41 per cent did not do so. As deferential support and authority slip from the reins of the state, the Government has tried to maintain some form of control by introducing 250 new closed circuit television (CCTV) schemes across the country, making the UK the Big Brother centre of the world[14] and further derobing the individual.

Demonstrators have more power than MPs, MEPs and CEOs. Institutions with the size and influence of the World Bank and the International Monetary Fund have been forced to cancel meetings and conferences as a direct result of the threat posed by anti-globalization protestors. Banks have pulled out of long-term multi-million pound loans to businesses in response to protests over activities such as scientific experimentation on animals.[15] This is of concern to businesses which, more than ever, must ensure that their purpose and processes are acceptable to an ever-growing body of stakeholders, a challenge to be explored further in Chapter 4.

The fuel protests of September 2000 illustrated the UK's arrival in the peoplist state with a resounding slap in the face for the most popular government since the Second World War. It signalled a shift from the pattern of the past when resolutions to disputes were thrashed out with a few all-powerful trade union leaders over beer and sandwiches at No. 10. Society has moved on. The distinction between the petrol protests and the disputes of the past is that power no longer lies in the hands of a few workers representing the many. Lorry drivers and small haulage company owners, farmers and taxi drivers did it for themselves. With the exception of a few mobile-phone calls and text messages between demonstrators, the protests and pickets were neither co-ordinated nor controlled. There existed no identifiable group with whom the Prime Minister could negotiate. This is the age of peoplism where, as we have witnessed, 'naked' individuals who are not members of trade unions or political groups can be extremely powerful.

Business consequences of disengagement from the state

Since the 1970s there has been a significant change in the traditional public/private sector split in service provision which favours the latter. Forward-thinking management should tackle the resulting concerns of workers over access to services such as health and education. State encouragement to join work-related pension schemes since the mid-1980s was an early indication of a trend rapidly gathering pace, although one that has now proved unsustainable as a result of other economic pressures. The logical extension of this trend may culminate in a wide range of measures offered by businesses as a substitute for current Welfare State provisions. Health cover and dental insurance are common contractual sweeteners. That human resources (HR) effectively capitalizes on concerns about the NHS and poor pension provision is widely recognized, but there exists the potential to push much further. If a company is trying to recruit a key knowledge worker who has concerns over his or her children's education, will the company offer to pay for private schooling? If the perceived benefits of recruiting a talented individual outweigh the costs, then basic economics indicate that it would. In such circumstances, wouldn't that worker think twice about leaving if their children were doing well at school? Progressive companies that realize the importance of their employees to their success will endeavour to clothe the naked individual by stepping in for the state where it is most needed.

During the agrarian and industrial revolutions, farmers and factory owners used tied houses to keep staff loyal. In the modern marketplace, and as globalization erodes the Welfare State, companies will utilize health, education, old age provision and an ever-widening net of benefits for workers and their families to tie some workers into a long-term commitment. Yet the cross-over in service provision goes further than the attraction and retention of workers. A vibrant professional-services sector relies on an adequate education system. If corporations do not believe that current education provision is satisfactory they will do one of two things: provide their own education or import skills on the global market from countries with a better education system. If companies are not getting the skilled workers they need – and there is a constant call from business in the UK to this effect – they will take a more direct hand in funding schools and universities so that they can have more enterprising individuals entering the job market. The demarcation between state provision and corporate investment is therefore likely to become even more blurred in the near future.

There are many examples of companies clothing individuals through benefits and perks. This approach is not new. What is interesting is that the types of support and help being offered are becoming more honed to the wider needs of naked individuals, in terms of support, encouragement and validation of personal goals. Land Rover offers non-job-related training to all employees, at a cost of £600 000 a year. Training requests have ranged from language training to taxidermy. This shows the desire of individuals to learn new skills in order to improve their employability. It also shows the recognition by their companies that they must facilitate such ambition.

One of the largest banks in Sweden, Swedbank, contributes money to improve the physical well-being of its staff. An example is its drive to encourage employees to give up smoking. The top 300 managers are allocated 5 days a year for 'reflection', an indication of the time and work pressures placed on co-members in the modern marketplace. In the search for meaning and support, HSBC bank has given its staff the chance to work alongside scientists from conservation charity Earthwatch on exotic environmental projects which range from tracking endangered jaguars in Brazil to researching the impact of humans on dolphins in Spain. Diageo encourages all co-members to meet external psychologists to develop personal 'life-plans', a facility designed to help balance work and personal goals.

Disappearing support structures

As we have seen, for the past few decades many of those able to afford it have opted out of state services such as health and education. Opting out of society is a trend gathering pace. Recent years have seen an increasing number of people choosing to live in gated communities. Cardiff alone is home to six inner-city gated communities which house up to 1000 people each.[16] Indeed, certain areas of London are already being privately policed by extra security funded by homeowners in the locality. There is a strong precedent from South Africa and the USA of a spiralling desire for individuals to lock themselves away. In the USA, more than eight million people live behind locked gates and, unsurprisingly, enquiries have soared since the terrorist attacks in 2001.

As a result of diminishing support structures, and an increase in self-serving behaviours, people are living alone for longer. Seven million people in the UK live alone. They account for around one-third of all households, and half of them are under pensionable age.[17] Another five million homes will be needed in the UK by 2010 to accommodate adults who wish to live on their own. The traditionally stigmatized label of 'spinster' will become a badge of honour, with carefree individuals able to afford hectic social lives and exotic holidays increasingly mocking of those restrained by dependants. In the near future we will associate more with people in our 'tribes' than our families. There are many social costs attributable to this evaporation of community. The rise in crime has been documented. The number of young people committing suicide has tripled over the past 30 years, and is now the second biggest killer of young men after car crashes. The Samaritans receive more than 5 million calls a year, up from 1.48 million in 1978.[18]

The clothing of the traditional family unit is becoming increasingly threadbare. Of all children born to married parents today, less than half will live in the same house as their father by the time they reach 16. Four in ten children are born to unmarried parents.[19] Families are decreasing in size, with the average birth-rate reduced to 1.74 children per woman. In 2014 the number of people aged 65 and over will exceed those aged under 65. Deaths will exceed births from the 2020s.[19]

Religion is constantly exposed to the ravages of scrutiny. Church attendances have fallen sharply during the 1990s. Christian churches in the UK shed almost 800 worshippers every Sunday. At the time of the agricultural and industrial revolutions, families of workers attended church in deference to their employers, who would note and act upon their absence. Without such pressure, and in an increasingly hectic and self-interested society, the future looks bleak for the Church. No longer can the instances of monetary misappropriation or social misconduct on the part of clergy members be hidden out of deference to the Church. Individuals are aware that they are in control of their own destiny and there is a palpable sense that the Church is no longer needed to shape their future. More people now consider themselves to be spiritual than religious.

The simple fact is, peoplism is no kinder than capitalism. Those without the skills prized in the people economy are the most challenged of the new era, and they will find it exceptionally difficult to survive in an economy that places a premium on talent above all else. It excludes those whose skills are outdated, who have been let down by inadequate education services, whose neighbourhoods are locked in a self-reinforcing cycle of deprivation, or who do not have the skills needed to navigate through an increasingly structure-less labour market. In the UK, 1.3 million adults and 140 000 18–21 year olds earn the minimum wage; 70 per cent of them are women.[20]

Fewer than one in five families are preparing adequately for a financially secure old age. Only 30 per cent of women and 40 per cent of men pay into a pension fund.[21] Final salary pension schemes are defunct.

Individuals will demand responsive, accountable and identi-fiable government. The state as we know it will have to change drastically in compliance. As choice is the currency in peoplist economies, we will witness an increase in gated communities, home-schooling and private policing. Not only will countries be prevented from raising taxes, but they will increasingly be pulled into a spiral of tax-cutting competition with other states attempting to attract and retain talented individuals. Nation states and companies will struggle to retain talented individuals, and struggle to support those who are not.

The thinking is ...

Organizations must be alive to the impact of naked individu-als on all aspects of their business so that they can:

- turn the threats posed by peoplism into opportunities for building commitment and motivation in individuals through innovative human resource strategies

- have a more targeted approach to attracting consumers, an area that will be examined further in Chapters 3 and 7. The naked individual forms a common link between demographic groups.

The reconciliation of two driving forces, firstly the fluid job market and lack of expectation of a job for life, and secondly the provision of non-work-related service provision, is a major challenge to modern business. The business implications of the naked individual are considerable. Corporate strategy must react to the new pressures being placed on co-members. In acting to clothe individuals, companies should create solid networks to help the naked individuals, such as instant peer groups and access to counselling lines. Similarly, companies must respond to the new rich by changing corporate attitudes to training, for which see Chapter 3, reward, as outlined in Chapter 4, and laying the foundations for 'venture peoplist' projects as detailed in Chapter 5.

As the nature of the relationship between state and citizen changes with the death of deference and an increased focus on management over leadership, so the nature of the relationship between employer and co-member evolves. This will be further analysed in the next chapter.

CHAPTER 2

The perils of disconnected thinking

The state is breaking down. Corporations are failing and insecurity is rife. This chapter examines the fundamental change-driver which is forcing companies to refocus and remodel: the changing nature of the 'employee'. This is the very essence of peoplism. It then analyses the litany of **_disconnected thinking_** corroding good management, illustrating how the co-ordination of business purpose and business practice can often break down.

The symptoms of peoplism are the empowerment of talent and the fluid economy. The consequences for business are that co-members have become fast, loose and fancy-free. Corporations are struggling to keep up because they are now entirely reliant on the quality and creativity of their employees, and human nature is the most unpredictable input of all. Talent moves at the speed of light, goes where it is welcome and stays where it is happy. Under capitalism companies were able to take a long-term view. The nature of the economy was such that stability was valued and steady growth was rewarded. The predictability of capital permitted accurate plans to be made years in advance. Peoplism renders such attempts futile. Long-term planning becomes irrelevant when the environment is in a constant state of flux. As a result, companies are forever walking on marbles, unable to achieve balance or stability. It is impossible to foresee the future with any accuracy.

The end of employees, the genesis of genius

Despite paying lip service to the business consequences of the creative economy, the attitude of many corporations towards their workers remains rooted in the past. A dichotomized outlook towards the value of executives and the value of the rest still permeates the culture of many businesses. This can be discerned from fragmented pay structures in which bosses value their talents as worth those of 212 shop-floor workers. However, the divisions and barriers which dissected companies under capitalism will soon be razed to the ground. Whatever else has been written about the dotcom phenomenon, it has brought about a permanent shift in the attitudes and expectations of talented co-members. The empowerment, self-awareness and ambition it has bestowed is sounding a death-knell to the concept of the subservient employee. Individuals are now valued for their creativity, innovation and enterprise skills. We are witnessing the end of 'employees' and the genesis of genius.

Top employees in the capitalist corporation were generally status driven. They were involved with providing an established service, avoiding risks and focusing on inputs. By contrast, peoplist co-members are defined more by their roles than by their positions. They have to be better team players and need an increased focus on speed to value, risk management and achieving outcomes. And, they know their worth.

As enterprising people become increasingly central to the creation of value, power has shifted perceptibly from employers and shareholders to many of 'their' workers. This is most obviously the case for the high-earning stars of the millennial labour market. Recruiting and retaining key workers is frequently identified as one of the main concerns of business leaders, including the CEOs of FTSE 100 companies. In the commodities marketplace, wisdom and human ability give advantage as creativity is required to develop goods and services sufficiently different to win market advantage (however short-term that advantage is). Ideas are the DNA of an organization and companies must develop a gene pool of talent able to add value across the business. A talent gene pool represents the skills and the qualities that are collectively offered by a company's co-members. Organizations should determine exactly what they want their gene pool to encompass, and actively recruit and test co-members to ensure a suitable match.

Success in business depends on organizations being able to build up a range of intangible assets, such as unique technologies, working methods and different ways of interacting with consumers. In turn, the development of these intangibles depends entirely on the creativity of co-members, from strategists drawing on information from around the globe, to front-line staff sharing their ideas for service improvement. People are the most important resource of any organization, and finding them, developing them and holding on to them becomes a nightmare.

Peoplism poses extreme challenges for the traditional functioning of business, and corporations will be crippled by the fact that their human talent is the ultimate mobile resource. Those with sought-after skills can work for *any* company in *any* city in *any* region in *any* country in *any* world(?)! As importantly, the interests of co-members are rarely aligned to company shareholder interests, which precludes the continuation of a narrow corporate focus on the latter.

Sensory overload

There is permanent discontinuity and uncertainty predominates. Information is available in excess, and protecting trade secrets proves exceptionally difficult, if not impossible. Innovative products can no longer dominate the market for long periods. Gillette spent US$750 million and 7 years developing a three-bladed razor, for which it charged a premium (as the first in market enjoys price premium). Within months Asda had an almost identical product on its shelves at a fraction of the price. Product cycles are shortening. The period that lapses from the breakthrough and innovation of a product or service, to its success, to commoditization as competitors catch up, to the resulting fall in prices and the need to innovate once more, has reduced significantly since the early 1980s. The 'shelf-life' of a product has taken on a new meaning. Success, too, is becoming short term, with many people achieving much more, much younger. The first to market gains a short-term price advantage, but in our age of instant information, others catch up quickly so the aim is to get in and sell out quickly.

It is easier for new players starting from scratch to develop new technologies, form new alliances and adopt innovative business processes, radically altering existing concepts and turning the tables on the old established players. It is the latter who will be challenged to keep up.

At an operational level the prevalence of information can cause dysfunction. The average manager receives more than 200 communications per day, of which 20 per cent are classified as important.[22] Users are becoming less patient with the internet. Today's online customer will wait just 8 seconds for a site to download before moving on[23] and the percentage of users unwilling to look beyond one page of search results has doubled to 50 per cent since 1997. The implications for companies with an online presence are clear; customer attention is increasingly difficult and expensive to attract, and to retain.

The speed with which businesses are able to respond and adapt to changes will determine the success or otherwise of each organization. It is therefore disturbing to read the results of a survey by the telecoms company BT, which showed that more than one-third of UK companies are not agile enough to react to economic and market upheavals (and BT should know!). A disturbing 35 per cent of the 450 British companies surveyed were not equipped to deal with the business implications of unexpected external world events such as terrorist attacks or foot and mouth disease. Seventeen per cent admitted they could not keep pace with changes in consumer habits, while 36 per cent were unable to react quickly to new overseas competition.[24]

Businesses must develop a culture that permits and encourages agile responses. The quickest application received for a job on reed.co.uk was 35 seconds from the job going live on the site. From the experience of running my own business, I have had direct experience of peoplism being 'fast, loose and fancy-free'. More than anything else, peoplism is fast. In 2000, one of our competitors announced that he had parted from his employer, had obtained some venture capital, and in 2 months would be launching an online temping agency. A couple of our young co-members said to us, 'Why the hell do they need two months? We could do that in a couple of weeks'. They did just that. After the announcement of our launch at a rather poorly attended press conference our market capitalization went up by £35 million – that was one-third of the capitalization of the company at the time – and we had not done anything except say that we were going to launch! Success in peoplism is going to be fast, but short as well. Within 12 months we had closed the venture with a £1 million loss.

Peoplism is loose. A few years ago, four members of the company set up a boutique recruitment specialism, which did exceptionally well, even making a profit in the second 6 months of its startup. I was delighted and went to congratulate the four before we all went home for the Christmas break. Upon returning after Christmas, the four had gone. They had simply realized that they did not need any protection from, or connection to, the company for the boutique to be successful. They had the skills and the knowledge to thrive just as easily on their own.

Peoplism is fancy-free. We find now that we have brilliant young people speeding up career ladders who suddenly come into the office and say – not, as they might once have said, that they have got a better offer (we make sure they do not get better offers now!) – that they want to go to South America for a year. Of course that individual is the boss now, so he or she goes to South America for a year, and comes back afterwards saying, 'What do you think about re-employing me?' We think that we would love to re-employ them, and so that is what happens. People are much more in charge of their own destinies now, and that is not such a bad thing. Companies should have an open-return policy for their valued people.

The pace of technological progress necessitates the need for speed in business. Agility and adaptability are key. Take the lesson of the chess showdown. In 1990 Gary Kasparov beat IBM's best chess computer, 'Deep Thought', in a highly publicized showdown. In 1996 there was a much-hyped rematch against IBM's 'Deep Blue'; the computer won one game, Kasparov was the victor in the remaining three matches. In the 1997 rematch Kasparov was roundly defeated by a machine capable of analysing thousands of moves simultaneously. Today, there is no human chess player who would stand even the remotest chance against a machine like the IBM computer, which can analyse more than 50 billion board positions every 3 minutes.[25] While computers will become increasingly agile and adaptable, for the time being they are not as creative as people, fortunately!

How to achieve optimum business agility

To achieve optimum business agility, companies must learn to think and act in double-quick time. This involves several steps, including developing a gene pool of talent, and ensuring that business processes and corporate culture permit maximum flexibility to empower all co-members to be responsive. One company where empowerment is a key value-driver is the hugely successful American domestic airline, Southwest Airlines. Even staff at low levels of authority are sufficiently entrusted to assume responsibility for what are often very important decisions. An example of the competitive advantage that can be achieved through empowerment came in 2000 when a competitor airline had to cancel a flight out of Dallas because of technical failure, turning away 100 passengers. A Southwest employee, with no express authority but with the implicit trust of the company, offered each passenger free membership to Southwest's frequent flyer programme and a free trip to their destination that evening. In effect, that co-member honoured the tickets of a competitor, something that would normally require a lot of paperwork and bureaucracy in other companies. What he did in practice was to react to exceptional circumstances and in the process gain 100 new passengers and members of the frequent flyer programme at a very small cost, since the airline had sufficient capacity on its flights to accommodate the extra passengers. Other key components for corporate agility which will be covered later in the book include having real-time communication strategies, keeping a close eye on consumer movements and developing a management dashboard.

Disconnect: Rethink: Connect

An appalling amount of disconnected thinking is evident in society and in business, resulting in dysfunctional business practice. Much of this dysfunctionality is attributable to organizational inflexibility and the inability of corporate leaders to treat co-members as the key-value drivers that they are. Too often these disconnections go undetected or un-abated. What follows is an exposé of some of the most corro-sive examples of disconnected thinking which are severely inhibiting EU plc. Remedies require an enterprising approach to the readjustments necessary in the people economy.

Disconnected thinking 1: Rewarding the wrong output

Too many companies pay people to come up with the wrong output. Organizational focus is often on sales as opposed to retaining clients. Customer satisfaction figures may be a far better indication of future sales than sales figures for one year. Concentration on shareholder return at the expense of other stakeholders' interests is supremely disconnected, and will be further examined in Chapter 4.

Disconnected thinking 2: Rash redundancies

For years we have witnessed crippling disconnected thinking from companies as they react to economic ebbs and flows. The point on the economic continuum when companies most need their key staff is in a downturn, yet all too often the bottom-liners pluck an arbitrary number of redundancies they deem to be necessary, and key talent is often lost. The situation is little better when voluntary redundancy is offered, as it will inevitably be the workers with the skills and the talent to find something else who will take advantage of the opportunity. Those who fear that their skills are of little value elsewhere will stay firmly put. As a result, companies end up in even direr straits, trying to navigate through uncharted waters having discarded their most capable crew. A survey showed that of 500 American companies that downsized between 1998 and 2001, fully one-third had, after downsizing, restored some previously eliminated positions.[26]

Companies must rethink. A BRMB survey commissioned in 2001 revealed that the vast majority of workers are more creative than their employers when thinking of alternatives to redundancy. One in five would accept a grant to take study leave, one in four would work reduced hours and more than one in ten would take unpaid leave to travel. Seven per cent would work for a charity until business picked up. The contrast is stark; most human resource departments are failing to think creatively and as a result come up with short-term, short-sighted fixes that do not solve their company's problems, in either the short, medium or long term.

Companies must ensure that they have a connected strategy. British Midland offered its pilots a choice when the company was hit in the downturn following the terrorist attacks in New York in 2001. Staff members were asked to work part time and to job-share in order to save more than 100 jobs. The expressed reason for the flexible approach was that, when the industry picked up, it would be easier for British Midland to expand by asking pilots to switch back from part-time to full-time working. It is in turbulent times that a company's true commitment to its people is tested. In addition, as people-sourcers in the most competitive industries in Silicon Valley can testify, downturns are often the best times to hire those with difficult-to-recruit skills. A short-term strategy may result in your key talent working for your competitors as markets pick up.

Disconnected thinking 3: Encouraging promiscuity

According to a study by OgilvyOne Worldwide, poor customer care is costing the top 10 per cent of businesses an estimated £15 billion a year in excess costs and lost revenue.[27] The difficulties of winning and retaining customers derive in part from the overcrowded supplier market of the people economy; customers have wide choices and competitors dedicate significant resources to stealing each other's customers. The paradox between intent and reality is also deliciously dangerous: suppliers invest in costly customer relationship management (CRM) systems to keep customers loyal while pumping more resources into prying customers away from competitors through special offers, reduced rates and other marketing tricks.

Companies should rethink. In essence, these companies are teaching consumers to be fickle, to be at liberty to shop around for the next best offer.[28] Supermarkets, mobile-phone producers and banks are all merrily participating in this vicious circle. So, while the rhetoric of companies in the peoplist economy is that they want loyal customers and loyal employees (note: they do not exist), companies actively encourage the opposite. This is just one more example of disconnected thinking to add to the list.

A connected strategy would suggest that the only way to guarantee success is for a business to ensure that it provides the best buy and the best service. Companies should give up trying to maintain indefensible positions.

Disconnected thinking 4: Half-brain power

By failing fully to engage women we are running the UK on half-brain power. Gender disparity in salaries starts soon after graduation. On average, women earn only 74 per cent of their male counterparts' salary.[29] Women hold only 10 per cent of boardroom posts. Just 24 per cent of managers in the UK are female.[30] Women in executive positions are outnumbered by 17 to 1. Only one CEO of a FTSE 100 company is female.

An organizational rethink is long overdue. However, the usual solutions and concerns proffered to tackle gender inequality in the workplace are too simplistic. Workplace dynamics are changing rapidly, and businesses big and small are failing to keep up. At a senior level, there needs to be a fair representation of stakeholders.

An ambitious example of a connected approach to gender equality is the San José National Bank in California. It has developed an innovative solution to the problem of staff retention among its largely female workforce with the introduction of its 'Babies in the Workplace' programme. The scheme goes beyond even the most innovative on-site daycare programme. With Babies in the Workplace, the newborn is not transported to an isolated crèche, but is completely cared for by the parent, who keeps the child in their office or work area. New parents are therefore encouraged to return to work sooner than they might otherwise, and are able to bring their babies back to work with them until the child is 6 months old or begins to crawl.

Parents taking advantage of the scheme must sign a strict liability waiver. There are drawbacks. If the baby cries during a meeting, both mother or father and child must exit. Other affected employees may request a 'baby-free' work environment, at their managers' discretion. If maternal and paternal stress has been a downside, the upside for the bank is higher productivity, lower absenteeism, especially amongst the parents, and higher morale. The move has also proved beneficial in a public relations sense, with an increased number of women opening accounts at the bank.

The rise in the number of computer-related positions makes the logistics of such policies easier. T3, a marketing firm in Austin, Texas, enticed a former key employee who had taken another job to return because he could bring his son along. As T3's Chief Executive articulates, 'Staff with babies at work will be distracted. Still, being here even at 60 per cent is better than totally missing that person. I would rather ease them back in and allow them to enjoy their family than have to completely retrain another person.'[31]

An excellent precedent has been set by IBM, who directly target women on maternity leave by offering a 25 per cent pay rise for those who return to work afterwards. People-friendly policies also do much to maintain low turnover levels and create a positive work culture in the organization. In comparison with an 18 per cent female workforce average in the IT industry, IBM benefits from a more balanced make-up of 30 per cent female staff. The company cites flexibility as the key, with offers of part-time work as well as pay rises encouraging nine out of ten employees who have left on maternity leave to return to the organization.[32]

A bigger-picture solution of connected thinking would be a tax-free allowance of, for example £10 000 per annum, for parents with children under the age of 10 to pay for childcare. We need more women in higher corporate positions, and we have to be more innovative and flexible in accommodating the fact that many talented women will choose to have children in addition to their careers. Connected, and radical, thinking is required to halt this dreadful waste of brain-power.

Disconnected thinking 5: An age-old problem

A similar lack of vision is responsible for the appalling amount of ageism which is cutting short the potential of a large proportion of the population. The 'lost generation' of the current labour market are men in their fifties. The employment rate for men aged between 50 and 64 is around 70 per cent, 10 per cent lower than that for the male work-force as a whole.[33] Ten per cent of firms have no employees over 50. The cost to the economy of this age discrimination is estimated at £31 billion.[34] More than a million people aged between 50 and 65 are economically inactive.

A rethink is required. The emphasis of the peoplist economy on creativity and enterprise skills means that age, at either end of the spectrum, is no longer a barrier to success. Employment should be tapered. Business simply cannot afford to ignore the pool of skills and experience among those who have left working life early. A recent study in the UK revealed that many more over-50s are capitalizing on their career experience to set up their own businesses. Older entrepreneurs were responsible for 50 per cent more start-ups in 2000 than in 1990, with almost 9000 businesses launched.[35] This figure is predicted to grow rapidly.

Employers must keep pace with social trends, and companies should have a connected approach to this issue. The fight for talent in the form of experienced, adaptable, flexible and hard-working individuals over the age of 45 is about to become a key focus for recruitment professionals. Already large employers are beginning to adapt to the changing demographic changes in the UK's labour market. Nationwide, for example, is overt in its attempts to tap into the skills that mature professionals have to offer.

Employers increasingly need mature workers and mature workers increasingly need employment. Decreasing state pensions, the volatility of private equity/employer-based pensions, increasing life expectancy coupled with earlier retirement, and the sheer psychological importance of work to individual evaluation of self-worth, mean that the view of retirement as the complete cessation of work is dying. In short, retirement no longer means withdrawal from the labour market, simply an adjusted reliance on the world of work for flexible income.

Disconnected thinking 6: Misdirected teachings

Companies would never invest the best of their talents and

experience to train direct competitors. Yet British universities go to enormous lengths to attract and teach overseas students. More than 10 per cent of undergraduates in the UK are from abroad. Around 85 per cent of London Business School's full-time MBA students come from overseas.[36] The situation arises in part because university coffers are £1 billion short each year of resources needed to keep buildings and equipment in working order.[37] As the Government continues to encourage greater attendance at universities, the costs of teaching British and EU undergraduates are covered by the marginal income made from postgraduate and overseas students. Although it is important to encourage the immigration of skills into the country, this is disconnected thinking as students from overseas are often preferred to domestic students because of the ways in which universities are rewarded. Since the early 1980s, the number of students in full-time education has doubled, while funding per student has halved. The share of spending on tertiary education in the gross domestic product of the UK is the lowest of any advanced country. If people are the most important resource, why is there so little investment into their development? There has been no real increase in the pay of university lecturers in the past two decades.

The preference for developing the skills of overseas students needs to be reassessed. This is a clear case of disconnected thinking at societal level, and one that pulls against the success of UK plc. The 'think local: act local' strategy should also apply to the development of the most important resources. Education is now a commodity market in which the UK should not compete internationally. Most students choose the UK to help them to learn how to speak English rather than because of any unique expertise on offer. Overseas students are charged a marginal rate and are getting a fantastic deal. The disconnection can also be seen in the USA, where the proportion of foreign students is much higher. This is leading to skills shortages in areas such as engineering, because too many PhD graduates leave to return home and do not continue to work in the USA.

Disconnected thinking 7: Brain harbour

For too long we have witnessed a bizarre, two-tiered approach to immigration and skills shortages in the UK. While locking up refugees and asylum seekers at our ports, irrespective of their skills and qualifications, we have pilfered doctors and nurses, technicians and labourers from the four corners of the world. Too many sources have made contradictory calls, demanding fewer immigrants while lamenting a lack of doctors in the National Health Service (NHS).

A rethink is required. Sufficient financial wealth has always been able to buy citizenship in any country. Now it should be a person's creative wealth, if anything, that permits such a choice. With an ageing population and a skills shortage spanning the employment spectrum, the logical progression of this common sense is not simply to sift through the PhDs in search of a select few people to plug the holes, but actively to recognize potential and to train immigrants ourselves.

If a nurse, engineer or cabinet maker has been forced to flee their homeland because of persecution, it is supremely short-sighted to allow that potential to be wasted when we are in need of such talent. Further, if a refugee or an asylum seeker has the *capability* to be a nurse, engineer or cabinet maker, why not train them in the country that will directly benefit from their skills? It is unfair to both the education and health systems of other countries when Western nations plunder thousands of nurses, teachers and police officers that they have trained. In doing so we have left countries such as South Africa and the Philippines drained of skilled workers that they themselves need.

Priority must be afforded to those with required skills, or those with the brain-power and ability to learn them quickly (not just ready-made professionals), although the Employability Forum and the Refugee Council estimate that as many as two-thirds of refugees are educated to degree level. The present blanket treatment of asylum seekers across Europe is expensive on different levels: the financial cost of the laborious asylum system, the cultural cost of precluded integration and, most importantly, the massive costs of wasted economic opportunity. In today's creative economy it is an imprudent price to pay.

Canada is an excellent role model for states facing acute skill shortages in the future. Its population of 31 million is ageing and the retirement of millions of baby-boomers will soon leave the country with a smaller and less skilled workforce. In response, the Canadian government uses its embassies and high commissions around the world actively to seek out new immigrants. Canada even sets an annual target for the number of new immigrants it wants to attract. When, in 2001, Canada attracted over a quarter of a million immigrants, 25 000 more than its target, it was seen as a cause for celebration and the new skills and talents were welcomed into the country.

Disconnected thinking 8: Dysfunctional charities

Charities are facing the wrong way in the people economy. In the past, charitable causes often focused on individuals with physical disabilities. The need for such help in the people economy is vastly reduced. For the winners in peoplism, those with portable enterprise skills, it matters not if they are in a wheelchair or registered blind as their talents rest in their minds. An increasing number of charities are sitting on growing funds unable to distribute grants through traditional avenues.

Charities will have to redraw the definitions radically as traditional needy causes disappear. With advances in medicine and technology, there will no longer be the same level of need for the traditional resources handed out by disability charities such as Guide Dogs for the Blind and Riding for the Disabled. However, as peoplism strips individuals bare, governments will struggle to manage those left behind. In the UK, the state has launched a scheme costing £40 million to give the long-term unemployed government-paid jobs. Launched in April 2002, the scheme is the first time that the government has met the full cost of providing jobs for the long-term unemployed.[38] This is indicative of the fact that in the peoplist economy those without the skills to survive will increasingly need special help. But how long can the government afford to be the crutch? While we already give money to the long-term unemployed via taxation, we may soon see direct giving via collecting tins and direct debits as charities reposition themselves to lend a hand to the losers in the people economy. There is still a great need for assistance in the people economy, but the leaks now come through a different part of the bucket, and it is those who do not have the skills to survive in the fast-paced economy who will suffer.

Disconnected thinking 9: Enterprise education

There is a constant cry from employers that graduate employees are ill-prepared for the world of work. Nothing is so important in the people economy as the need for a spirit of enterprise to be encouraged and promoted throughout all aspects of the economy, from schools and universities to business leaders and politicians.

Both the government and companies need a rethink: enterprise is required everywhere. It is not about creating hundreds of Richard Bransons. Enterprise is about an attitude, a can-do spirit fuelled by creativity, communication and original thought. True, some individuals will use their enterprise skills to become entrepreneurs, but enterprising people are desperately needed in the private, public and voluntary sectors.

Enterprise must be introduced at the heart of lessons and lectures to prepare young people for the new challenges of the workplace. Enterprise skills are about empowering and tooling up individuals to survive and thrive in the continually changing job market. There needs to be an enterprise thread that carries on from school to university to working life (for enterprise training in business, see Chapter 3). *Enterprise learning* should be adopted as a way of delivering each of the subjects on the national curriculum, as a style of teaching and learning as well as a subject in its own right. Team building, creative problem solving and self-management should be at the heart of all lessons. The ability to tackle problems, take the initiative, be flexible and work effectively alone and with others, is crucial to success.

A Disconnected Thinking Audit may be of use in your organization (see the box overleaf). It is content dependent on the particular types of disconnected thinking that threaten optimum performance in each company. Thus, the tool should be tailored to each individual company, and refreshed as relevant.

The thinking is ...

Business leaders must be alive to the implications of disconnected thinking in wider society, since business continues to encroach ever further into traditional areas of government responsibility. Using lateral thinking to identify ways in which disconnections in national and global strategy can be better connected is good conditioning for business leaders. Conducting a 'disconnected thinking audit' is the first step to ensuring your business is moving forward with a joined-up strategy. Many of the old rules no longer apply, and the pace with which current thinking will evolve is only going to increase. Companies must be conscious of the possibility that aspects of process and procedure are, or may become, disconnected. Forward-thinking managers will act to reconnect immediately.

Disconnected thinking audit

Rewarding the wrong output

■ What are your core organizational aims?

■ What do you want your people to prioritize/produce?

■ What is your system of reward based on?

■ Does this system support your core aims?

■ If not, how can you realign reward to encourage your people to work towards these core aims?

Rash redundancies

■ Do you have contingency plans for the event of an economic downturn?

■ If these involve redundancy, how will you ensure that you retain your key talent?

■ How do you plan to cope with economic recovery in terms of staffing levels?

■ Do you need to:
  ❑ Consider creative options to redundancy? What other options could you offer?
  ❑ Exchange your short-term fixes for long-term recovery?

Half-brain power

■ What is the gender balance in your organization?

■ How many women do you have in senior positions?

■ How well does their remuneration compare with that of men?

■ Is long-term retention of women an issue for your organization?

■ What percentage of your workers are over 45?

- Does your organization have a youth culture that under-utilizes the wisdom of your older workers?
- Have you examined your work–life balance policies to ensure that you are doing all you can to keep your key workers satisfied?

CHAPTER 3

The dysfunctional corporation

Many corporations are dysfunctional because they permit out-of-date management structures and organizational objectives to inhibit optimum business performance. This chapter advocates the reorganization of management structures, the refocusing of executive training and the redirection of the current business obsession with branding into *badge* development. Executive positions have become too big for individuals, causing underperformance, inefficiency and chaos in the majority of companies, and death and destruction in a minority, such as Railtrack and the National Health Service. The speed and nimbleness demanded of businesses is driving devolution through the heart of organizational structures. In addition, despite the lazy rhetoric that brands wield unrivalled power, a narrow focus on brand values is unwise. Pouring money into the development of brands is dysfunctional, as they are being attacked on four fronts: from extremely well-informed consumers, from increasingly powerful competitors, from ceaseless technology and from omnipresent creativity. This in turn has serious implications for the future of marketing.

Jobs are too big for people

The leaders and senior executives of large organizations cannot cope. Jobs have become too demanding for individuals, and chief executives and directors across the Western world are resigning, or being fired, at an unprecedented rate. A trend of serial resignation is evident. While this book was being written, no fewer than 37 directors, chief executive officers (CEOs) or chairmen handed in their resignation or were sacked. Reasons ranged from apparent financial mismanagement to lack of performance.

The average life span of a CEO is now less than 3 years, and falling.[39] One in four CEO appointments ends with the appointee resigning from the post before the contract expires.[40] A survey of 30 European CEOs of multinationals such as Nestlé and Unilever revealed a deep fear of failure and concerns over leadership style. Interestingly, only 2 of the 30 had been groomed for the position of CEO, highlighting the rapid rate of CEO turnover and a lack of succession planning.[41] Individuals are getting appointed to top positions earlier in their careers.

Jobs are too big for many others besides the top dogs, and according to recent research, more than 70 per cent of newly hired executives leave within the first 2 years.[42] The problem is not just in the boardroom: of the 92 English league football teams only five can boast managers who have been in the job for 5 years or longer. Only 18 have managers with 2 years under their belt. Here too, jobs are, quite simply, too big for individuals. This is the simple explanation as to why there

are so many high-profile resignations across such a broad
spectrum, at a time when CEO salaries are rocketing. The
duties of the CEO are changing at an unprecedented rate.
Part of the problem is that success is often measured in
terms of shareholder value, a fickle measurement which is
heavily dependent on market forces at any given time.
Delivering shareholder value has become the Holy Grail
of corporate management and as a consequence other
indicators of good management have fallen by the wayside.
Focusing on one indicator increases temptation and makes
for easier manipulation of success, as we have witnessed with
some of the American accounting scandals. Of greater
complicity is the fact that workloads are becoming
increasingly complex and the political, economic, bureau-
cratic and market considerations of the knowledge economy
are too demanding. Commoditization and the erosion of
margins mean that tight costs and price pressures further
restrict the manoeuvrability of business leaders. There has
been a significant fall in job satisfaction,[43] and the reasons
why more people in the UK work longer hours is that the
jobs themselves are becoming increasingly demanding, with
83 per cent of those working long hours doing so in order to
meet deadlines and pressures.[43]

For many executives feeling the heat, there is little incentive
to stay when the going gets tough. Golden goodbyes and
payoffs provide soft landings (Lord Simpson of Marconi
provides a high-profile example). A further conclusion
drawn from this roll call of resigners is that in the executive
landscape transferable skills allow individuals to switch to
another job almost painlessly. After the dotcom frenzy fizzled
out, many of the executives who had left large organizations

either to set up or to become involved in start-up companies were reintegrated into the corporate fold. Their experiences were viewed as helpful not harmful in the long term. Failure is not viewed so harshly as it once was, and is often seen as a helpful stepping stone to bigger and better opportunities. One example is Gerald Corbett, who failed as a leader (in the eyes of the public, although not necessarily in the eyes of the shareholders) at Railtrack before leaving and landing a powerful new job at Kingfisher.

Test for, and train in, enterprise skills

While the nature and demands of management have changed significantly in recent years, the attitude of business leaders has been surprisingly slow to keep pace. We are still witnessing the pattern of the past whereby those who are good at their job are plucked out into management, robbing classrooms of the best teachers, marketing departments of their best thinkers, laboratories of their best researchers and so on. These actions, which are slowly being halted in the public sector with the introduction of super-nurses and advanced skills teachers, have reinforced for years the notion that management is neither a specialism nor a skill set, but an add-on for experienced co-members.

It is apparent from the cascade of resignations that we are still recruiting to an old organizational model. Current employees have been educated and trained under a capital model where a gaggle of qualifications and certificates was thought sufficient to cope with the demands placed on individuals. With the dynamic pace of change, these no longer hold such relevance. Employees should be selected on their enterprise skills, on their creativity and innovation, their abilities to solve problems and create opportunities. Intuitive intelligence is the benchmark at Reed, and co-members must show they have it before they are rewarded with responsibility. The key point is that everyone needs to be enterprising. In practice this means that everyone needs to have some form of enterprise education to be better able to ride the waves of change. For those already in the workplace, training in enterprise skills should be the priority for the HR department, even before job-specific training. It is clear that we must all learn a new game.

Forget company, think enterprise

Testing for enterprise skills is difficult, but necessary. A strategic approach to integrating enterprising behaviours should be adopted, beginning as early in the work-cycle of the co-member as possible. Ask candidates at interview what the best idea they have ever had is, and see what kind of answer you get. Generally such a question is met with an embarrassed titter. A common question asked to candidates at a major computer corporation is to quantify how much water runs through the Mississippi River. It is not a specific quantity that is desired as an answer, but enterprising ideas on how to obtain the information.

If your company has several operating divisions or departments, why not change the focus for a limited period for 5 per cent of the operation to generate ideas that might improve the performance of the company as a whole? Draw up a timetable and set targets to redirect teams and departments away from operational matters, on an alternating basis. Depending on your business, this could be done during the fallow period (or 'down times'). For Reed, and a lot of service industries, December is a quiet month, for others it will be August or July. Why not rename it 'creative month' and refocus the minds of those who know the operation best on how radically to improve the business.

Record and benchmark how many ideas each division and each employee has had, what improvements have been made to specific operations, and what ideas have contributed to the whole operation. For an organization to be enterprising, it is imperative that these things are measured. One way to do this is to develop Profit:Enterprise Ratios, which is further explored in Chapter 6.

At Reed we have a strategically 'quick and dirty' ideas scheme on the company intranet, called ReedThink. It is budgeted for within the company and sets high targets for each operating company to award money for innovative ideas. We deliberately give the money before ideas are proved or adopted, to show that if a co-member provides the idea, we will provide the award and adopt the risk of whether it works or not. This is important: divorcing the execution of the ideas from their creators reinforces the value of ideas and innovation in and of themselves, and encourages enterprising behaviour throughout the organization.

It is also up to us as individuals to make sure that enterprise training is a prerequisite before accepting a new position. We are in control of our own destinies and are responsible for ensuring that companies invest in our employability. Co-members should be able to choose their own training, providing they can show the direct relevance to the company, although enterprise training is relevant to all organizations. Enterprise training will soon become the new hook for companies to attract and retain innovative employees: out with private health insurance, in with private intellect insurance!

Executive triangles

In addition to the need for a greater emphasis on enterprise skills, an immediate solution to the problem of jobs being too big for individuals is to create more duet or trimeric positions. Two heads are better than one. There are numerous examples of the truth in this old adage, from Rolls-Royce to Marks & Spencer, Procter & Gamble to Hewlett Packard, Hanson & White to the Barclay brothers. Three heads are better still. By creating a top team of three individuals working simultaneously on three positions, businesses may see success where individuals have failed. Forming a triumvirate represents an apex of control, and prevents eyeball-to-eyeball confrontations between the chairperson and the CEO, leading to greater acquiescence and better outcomes. Such a strategy recognizes that organizations now need different strengths in leaders. This realization is not a new one, and the desirability of triumvirates as a leadership structure has been set from the dawn of creation, with the Hindu Trinity of Brahma, Vishna and Shiva, the Egyptian Trinity of Khepri, Horakhty and Atum, and the Christian trinity of the Father, Son and Holy Ghost, not to mention the Roman triumvirates of 60 BC with Julius Caesar, Marcus Crassus and Pompey the Great, and of 43 BC of Mark Anthony, Octavian and Lepidus. In modern business, different strengths are required for different aspects of leadership, whether for integrating a merger, successfully managing a company or implementing change. The business landscape changes so quickly in the life of an organization that the 'fit' of an executive is neither desirable nor attainable. The senior management at Shell is in effect run on a committee of six leading executives. Such a system is more appropriate to the people economy; the autocratic style of senior management typified by organizations such as GEC is no longer the best way to produce results in today's complex markets or, indeed, to retain leaders.

There are four or five roles from which a triumvirate should be drawn. These include the CEO, the chairperson, the chief operating officer, the chief financial officer and the head of human resources.

Bolster your boss

Bolstering your boss requires the development of an integrated strategy for top- and middle-level management which includes executive coaching, succession planning and developing goal-orientated performance-related pay (see Chapter 4 on the last). It is important that structures are put in place whereby problems can be flagged up quickly and the wider pool of co-members is encouraged to manage their boss. Perhaps workers should be measured on how well their boss does, to encourage the development of a strong number two for all the key positions.

Lesly Higgins is an independent executive coach in Silicon Valley. The most common issue that she sees is that of senior managers in jobs that are bigger than they have ever had, having to shift from being personally involved in delivering results to delivering results through others. Such executives are often managing others, yet have no experience of coaching or delegation. Her mission is to help people to enhance the skills they already have, to be clear about where they are effective at work and to provide ongoing support. She facilitates growth within an organization.

The trend in coaching in the USA is to insist upon 360-degree feedback, preferably through one-to-one interviews. In presenting such feedback to the executive it is possible to see clear themes in terms of performance and, equally importantly, in terms of perception. It is difficult for executives to shrug off criticism when they can see it written in their employees' own words. Such feedback increases the awareness of where they need to go.

The executive coach will then co-create a development plan, agree on a set number of primary areas to be addressed (usually three) and design practices that will help to build the appropriate competencies. Understanding the gap and knowing how to bridge it are tremendously important for individuals struggling to cope in their positions. One client was an internet executive who readily admitted his inter-personal skills were poor when he felt under stress. The feedback showed that this was more of a problem than he had originally thought, with the likelihood that it was leading to key staff leaving the organization. Upon closer exploration with Lesly, it transpired that it was the fear that his job was too big which was leading to this stress. Therefore, the practices that Lesly implemented were grounding practices, such as increasing exercise and meditation, and not merely practices designed to boost communication skills, which might have been a surface solution.

One further solution to jobs being too big for individuals is to make the jobs smaller, which can be accommodated through encouraging greater devolution in organizational structures.

Peoplism drives devolution

The smaller the company the bigger the car

This is an era when bigger is definitely not better. Multinational corporations may soon be a thing of the past as the sloth of the supertanker is superseded by the speed of the jet-ski. New organizations are increasingly using novel organizational structures to establish strong global positions quickly. Traditional multinational corporations will struggle to keep up with the more nimble companies that make greater use of the internet-based networks to connect to customers and clients. Indeed, such companies will be weighed down by their capitalist trappings, and overtaken by more peoplist-centric companies. The business environment of tomorrow is more pluralistic and diverse. In an age when speed of innovation and communication are imperative, devolution is a connected approach to strategy and decision making.

The size and nature of organizations have become key concerns of top management, and are now inextricably bound up with strategy formation.

The diversity of modern markets, particularly in terms of consumer groups and business clients, has eroded the utility of strong centralized managerial structures. A key driver of success is the degree of closeness with clients and customers, and the ability to develop relationships and react to changing needs and desires. This relationship building is carried out at ground level, and information gathered is able to flow upward to decision makers as the stimulus of policy formulation. Consequently, hierarchies of control have to be relaxed with an accompanying flow of authority down the corporate ladder.

Structural devolution motivates individuals to take ownership of their ideas and the process of organizational development. The huge number of skilled professional workers who left their steady, well-paid jobs to join start-up companies at the beginning of the dotcom boom spoke just as much of their frustration with the lack of personal control and organizational influence as of their desire to accumulate wealth. Devolution can act to liberate talent, innovation and ideas otherwise hidden or weighed down within traditional corporate structures. Freeing people to drive business forward is now the goal towards which all companies must strive. This process should begin with a reassessment of corporate structures, business processes, and reporting and accountability channels.

In 2000, Reed took these principles on board with an internal 'starburst' restructuring of the company's operations. The aim was to devolve greater power to our co-members and ensure that the company was as close as possible to its customers in the numerous markets in which we compete.

Starburst has succeeded in pumping new energy into the company. The five operating companies – Reed Learning,

Reed in Partnership, Reed Solutions, Reed Connections and Reed Personnel Solutions – that were established in the devolution process are able to keep a closer eye on industry trends, a characteristic that has served us well in uncertain economic times. Reed Executive plc, the holding company, still retains ultimate care of the company's star performers, but the restructuring has allowed the focus on strategy development to fall at a company-by-company level. The strategy has even gone one step further, with Reed Healthcare plc, one of the operating companies, being demerged from the group in 2001 and achieving its own quote on the London Stock Exchange. This reshaped the ownership of the company, going beyond the devolution of responsibility. Delegation of responsibilities is never easy, but the rewards have been clear, creating a more focused organization and freeing up time and energy in Reed Executive's senior management, who are now able to take a more holistic overview of the group's trading activities.

A case in point: Abbey National

Abbey National, a UK-based bank, has launched a trial franchise scheme with 48 branches participating. The aim is to transfer elements of the business into the hands of the franchisee, including decision making on opening hours and product offering. While still a trial, it is apparent that Abbey National and other organizations are beginning to recognize the need to try out new systems of management and control in order to be more responsive to customers and flexible with co-members. While giants such as McDonalds and Coca-Cola have also divested control from above, the industry in which these companies operate supports that type of business strategy, since food and drink production usually occurs in the country of origin. However, a financial services organization leading the way in allowing greater independence to aspects of its business is more indicative of peoplism. Abbey National, which has over 750 branches, began the first franchise pilot programme in August 2000.

Retail banking is an industry that has become increasingly competitive over recent years, with the large supermarkets and internet banks entering the market. Abbey National has been experimenting with a number of different ways to change the whole approach to the delivery of retail banking services. These have included a partnership agreement with Costa Coffee, which saw the establishment of in-branch coffee shops open to customers and non-Abbey customers alike. Behind the concept was a desire to buck the national trend of branch closures and revitalize the existing network, and to make the branches more welcoming.

Franchising takes Abbey's commitment to innovation a step further and was adopted to make the company more responsive and adaptable. The project, which has shown early signs of success, is now being rolled out in more areas. The scheme has encouraged innovation and creativity among all levels of employees, helping to revitalize the branch network. One employee, a customer relationship manager, recently proposed a novel way of encouraging sales using the idea of a Monopoly board. Each branch is allocated a Monopoly piece (hat, car, etc.), with the aim of achieving the highest sales possible. At the end of each week, the four teams that have the most money pass 'GO' and collect a luxurious hamper each.

Franchising signals a change to the relationship between branch employee and branch management, and between branch management and Abbey National's central management. The franchisees have taken the place of what were formerly area managers. Each potential franchisee is obliged to 'bid' for an area or 'market'. In most markets, other managers will be involved in the bidding process, which involves devising a new, ambitious business plan. Each franchise manager takes on a market consisting of six to nine branches, and is granted far greater autonomy in the running of the market than they would be under central Abbey control.

The benefits are clear. Franchisees have control over smaller numbers of branches than was previously the case for area managers, allowing more time to be spent on specific branch improvement. Added to this, franchisees have a greater degree of flexibility in the way they manage staff and run the business, a freedom that has been especially beneficial to Kevin Bracey, franchisee in the Enfield and Harlow market. Through the franchising arrangement signed with Abbey after having his bid accepted, Kevin has taken a 25 per cent pay cut to his basic salary. In return, he is able personally to retain (and divide among his staff) profits over and above his targets laid down in his initial franchise business plan. This offers the possibility of his salary being tripled.

Kevin has enjoyed the freedom to recruit new staff members in the form of a training manager who looks specifically at the changing skill sets required on the branch floor, as well as a personal assistant to take over the administrative tasks that previously took up much of his time. Kevin has seized the opportunity to strengthen his management team, and there are now 12 managers covering his eight-branch market, instead of the company ratio of one per branch.

Clearly, one of the primary benefits of the franchising agreement is the latitude given to individual franchisees to innovate on service delivery. Kevin took the opportunity to market the branch in response to World Cup fever in the summer of 2002. With his new flexibility he was also able to close the branches during important England matches, a goodwill gesture to members of staff that would not have been possible under more centralized management control. 'Fun days' were organized in which each employee wore a different football shirt for one day during the World Cup, and the interior décor of each branch was decked in football paraphernalia. This day bore tangible results to the bottom line: the local network sold as many new instant credit accounts in a day as would normally be expected in a week.

Franchising has been welcomed in Abbey by a new generation of middle managers, whose spirit of entrepreneurism and creativity might otherwise have been stifled under too much central control. The local market controlled by Kevin Bracey has propelled itself from 84th position in Abbey's performance tables to 33rd, in just 3 months, and all of the pilot franchise programmes are considered a success. Above all else, franchising has served to unlock more of the creative potential of the company's management that had previously been trapped within layers of middle management and over-standardized central control.

Smaller units with greater devolved control can move more quickly, allowing the organization to maintain pace with its competitors. They are more efficient and more responsive. What were previously mass-markets are becoming fragmented micro-markets, placing significant pressures on businesses to pander to increasingly choosy consumers.

The death and destruction of brands

Brands are one of *the* hot topics in business. Some of the most established and heavily endorsed brands are attached to obvious commodities such as beer, soap and tobacco. Companies have spent billions lifting their brands out of these commodity markets in order to charge a premium for a product that is virtually identical to that of a competitor.

While innovation and new product development permit short-term benefit, a powerful brand image can, in theory, lead to a long-term competitive advantage by inspiring customer loyalty. However, in reality, brands are under attack, and are no longer able to provide sustainable advantage. So begins the rise of the badge; in essence, a brand that spans multiple products and services.

Brands emphasize the evolving distinction of the product, while badges emphasize the distinction of the producer or the supplier. Badges encompass the rise of the branded workplace where targeting internal customers (co-members) is as important as targeting external customers. Each product or service produced or provided by the company is clearly labelled as being produced or provided by that company. The ultimate badge is Stelios's 'Easy' emblem, which is involved in a range of sectors including transport, internet cafés, hospitality, hire cars and now finance. The 'Easy' badge was built up from air travel and is now exploited expertly in other highly competitive markets. There is a continuum between brands and badges (Figure 1). Very few of either fall wholly into one camp or the other, and most occupy a point somewhere in between. As the impact of peoplism takes

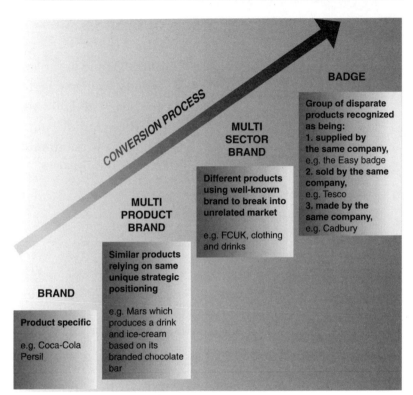

Figure I   From brand to badge.

greater hold in the economy there will be a more concerted move from the former towards the latter. This can be evidenced most recently by Unilever, which has embarked on a stated policy to refocus its strategy away from the brands it owns, and onto itself as a badged producer.

There are three types of badge:

■   *The point-of-delivery badge*, such as Tesco, is a very wide badge. Tesco can add any number of unconnected products under that badge, from milk to rat poison to whisky to stockings to banking to insurance. In this type of badge, the consumer trusts the badge owner to be a purchaser on their behalf. For example, I know that the own-label produce I purchase at Sainsbury's is not made in-house, but I trust the values and the standards of the badge owner to make a good choice on my behalf. The badge owner becomes the buyer of choice for the consumer.

■ *The point-of-origin badge*, such as Cadbury, involves products being badged by the manufacturer. Cadbury could bring out a chocolate bar every week and it would stand a better chance of success than a new narrow brand because consumers would trust the quality of the badged manufacturer. This is not as wide as the point-of-delivery badge as they can only manufacture products of a similar nature. Cadbury's detergent or cheese would not be an option.

■ *The service badge*, for example the 'Easy' badge, gives an indication of the drivers of the service provision. In this case those drivers would be efficiency, low cost and no frills. There is a very wide opportunity to provide services. One could imagine the Easy badge being opened up to a number of alternatives.

Narrow brands have to spend an increasingly disproportionate amount of money on marketing, in an effort to retain a half-decent market share from new competitors. Coca-Cola's exorbitant $150 million paid for the global marketing rights to the Harry Potter films is indicative of the huge amounts of money needed to buoy up the big brands. Yet money can no longer guarantee success, as Coca-Cola learnt from its expensive, yet unsuccessful, attempts to make an impact on the Russian market.

We are witnessing the beginning of a trend that will see the strength of brands dwindle. Brands are under attack on four fronts:

- Customers are no longer prepared to pay inflated prices to support brands.

- Competitors and badge owners are increasingly able to produce an almost identical product with lower development costs, and without having to spend fortunes trying to protect brand domination.

- Technology makes the position of brands precarious as it facilitates easier and cheaper market entry and makes protecting trade secrets practically impossible.

- The drive for creativity in product development and service delivery threatens the established positions of stagnant brands that have little else than their reputation to rely on.

In the age of corporate social responsibility and the clued-up consumer, substance is all-important over style. There is considerable weight of opinion that one of the reasons the dotcom bubble burst was that the marketeers concentrated too much money and time on brand-building without ensuring that their systems and offerings were in order. (Two such proponents are Charles Mcleod, founder of 4Less Group, and Bruno Rost of Experion.[44])

Singular brands, no matter how well established, are at risk from evolving badges. As a result, brands cling on to other company's brands in an attempt to stay afloat. The affiliation between McDonalds and Coca-Cola smacks of a kind of producer protectionism. Functioning as a badge requires a coherent marketing strategy across the whole organization, as contradictions and conflicts between products must be avoided. However, because the values are consistent, costs can be kept to a minimum and the success of a product or service in existing markets can be exploited when the time comes to expand into new markets or product areas. The most obvious disadvantage of badges is that problems with one product may have a greater impact on the performance of the company's other products. It remains to be seen what impact the recent problems experienced by Virgin Rail will have on the performance of the rest of the Virgin Group. Companies should be cautious about over-zealous cross-marketing as it can damage their badge. This occurs when consumers approach a company for a specific service, and ancillary services are foisted upon them. This cross-selling is becoming commonplace in many industries as the fight for consumer attention intensifies, and banks are particularly guilty of this practice.

In the capitalist economy, the big brand owners were able to dictate the volume and positioning of the products into the stores. Now, with the rising importance of the badge, the tables have turned and the supermarkets, which are very much badge owners, can call the shots with the brand owners.

To retain market share, brands are not merely about selling goods, but have become about selling an ideal. This is why it is necessary to have a corporate refocus on badges. Individuals have unlimited access to real information and are no longer interested in aspirational advertising or brands which attempt to convince them that the world will change if they buy a particular product. Young consumers are seen to have a dislike for homogeneity and a preference for the quirky and diverse. The values behind badges will become more important than the slogans behind brands. In the information age the badged corporate story will overshadow a product and its shiny image: traditional brands beware.

Prioritize PR

To be successful badge owners must be good at getting attention. As companies move from branded products to badged outputs it becomes increasingly difficult to deliver a coherent advertising message. Badges succeed on the concepts that they represent, such as the key values of no-frills and efficiency within the Easy empire. It is much easier to relay these values, which imbue several different services, through public relations (PR) activity, than through a 30 second advertisement.

PR should be prioritized over advertising, as it is a much more effective form of familiarizing consumers with your company values and your products. In the not too distant past it was considered mind-blowing marketing to have a corporate brochure. Then came the corporate video, the website and the CD Rom. In Reed we have used all of these things but they are cursory; what one needs to concentrate on providing is the best product or the best service, and if you can do that, you should get as much PR exposure as possible.

An excellent example of prioritizing PR is the irrepressible Sir Richard Branson, who has built up his Virgin badge through an endless series of PR stunts. These have included widespread media coverage of the businessman careering into the sea in a badged hot-air balloon, dressing up in a tight-fitting wedding dress, strolling around Trafalgar Square accompanied by nude models and being hoisted up American offices in a naked body-suit while standing on a huge mobile phone.

Naturally, PR can be both positive and defensive. The negative coverage that British Gas received in the press in June 2002 for intimidating customers to cancel arrangements in order to be at home for meter readings has caused damage that any future activity will have to work hard to heal. There is no hiding place in the people economy for disrespectful or arrogant behaviour. The 'Gerald Ratner' factor can alienate even the most loyal of customers and employees, and destroy a thriving business. Technology has fuelled the speed and success with which disgruntled customers can cause harm to companies, with the plethora of websites dedicated to venting wrath at 'ntl' providing a good example. New communications technology and a growing awareness of the actions of corporations have enabled this kind of information to reach the mass media and the individual consumer.

As news increasingly becomes a commodity there is an insatiable demand for stories. Therefore, publicity and PR are more cost-effective, and easier, to master than ever before. Within Reed we have tracked the impact on visits to our website prompted by stories about the company in the press. Even less than flattering exposure will see the number of page impressions increase by anywhere between 5 and 10 per cent, and that has to be a good thing overall.

Blow-pipe marketing

The main component of PR and blow-pipe marketing, that is one-to-one marketing, involves companies having a strong badge to encourage both co-members and consumers to self-select. This has long been the case with ethically branded businesses such as The Co-operative Bank and The Body Shop, which set out their values very clearly and invite consumers to choose them. This is likely to become the case in many other sectors as well, as companies accept that there is little point marketing to broad groups, and it is much more prudent to attract smaller groups of sympathetic consumers whose potential profitability is higher. In the past there was a blunderbuss approach to marketing; the idea was to hit as many people as possible with your business message and hope that some targets were struck. Now it is prudent to specialize your PR and customer retention strategies to different tiers of customers according to their customer loyalty value. This is an echo of smart human resource management strategies which ensure that those employees who add the most value are most vigorously sought and retained.

The thinking is ...

While it is conceded that in a hangover from the 1990s the market share and influence of leading brands remain powerful, peoplism has rendered the foundations unsafe. Instant consumer knowledge, increased consumer choice and the demise of both customer and co-member loyalty are shaking the dominance of brands. The greater the number of individuals taking advantage of the increased choice available in the people economy, the greater the concern for companies that rely heavily on established and fixed branded products. Companies must instead develop and live their badge; it should be detectable in everything from product innovation to human resource policies to public relations campaigns. A similar peoplist refocusing is required for organizational structure and management charts. Jobs are too big for people because of the frenetic pace of the economy and our obsession with early specialization in business, and devolution of responsibility is an excellent way to liberate the key economic value driver: talent.

CHAPTER 4

Inside out

Business attitudes have had to evolve dramatically in the people economy. This is partly because of the increased transparency of information and partly due to a growing awareness by individuals of their own importance as co-members and consumers. Consequently, stakeholder power is more influential than at any time. The traditional hierarchy of priorities, descending from shareholders to customers to employees to the wider community, has expired. However, a staggering number of companies still suffer from being complacent in their success. This chapter probes beyond the extravagant examples of corporate arrogance, such as Gerald Ratner's insulting views on his own company's products and Halifax Building Society's disrespectful views on the types of account holders that they would prefer to avoid. It outlines how a lack of focus in business procedures can work against corporate success, and can create a dangerous level of organizational complacency.

Avoiding arrogance involves an in-depth examination of internal business processes, market direction and human resource (HR) strategies. This chapter details how best to cope through a combination of added-value estimates and unique strategic positioning (USP).

CSR: 'corporate spin in reality'?

Corporate social responsibility (CSR) has evolved in response to the pressures for meaning, accountability and direction placed upon companies by naked individuals (in the form of customers and co-members). The response by the vast majority of companies, however, has been distinctly capitalist. CSR is a conceptual catch-all, encompassing sustainable development, corporate citizenship, business ethics, environmental concerns, contribution to society, treatment of employees and so on. The new triple bottom line symbolizes the social, ethical and environmental objectives which are becoming as important as the financial measurements so narrowly focused upon in the past.

The business case for a clear and concise CSR strategy is heartening. There have been around 80 studies to date into the impact of CSR programmes on businesses. Of these, 42 showed a positive impact, 19 found no link, 15 produced mixed results and only four showed a negative impact.[45] An independent cost–benefit analysis in 2001 estimated that The Co-operative Bank's environmental and ethical policy accounted for between 15 per cent and 18 per cent of its pre-tax profits.

The ethical concerns of business cannot be separated from those of society at large. For organizations involved in industries where there are known user-addiction problems, the growing ethical expectations of society have a major effect. The UK Government is seeking to force gambling companies to invest a sum to treat gambling addicts.[46] This is a foolish move in the people economy, as those companies with a solid online presence will simply move offshore. Any moves in this direction must be organization or consumer led, not imposed by jurisdictional regulatory authorities.

A cursory glance at the companies that consistently come top of polls of the best employers and the most admired companies reveals that, for most commentators, CSR is an important component for attracting and retaining committed co-members. A strong CSR policy can be a good retention tool for companies; Mike Hodgkinson, the CEO of BAA, describes the company's low staff turnover as 'the mark of a company whose employees are motivated and understand the company and share its objectives'.[47] In the talent wars, top talents are more likely to choose a firm that reflects their concerns about society. This is especially true for graduate and younger applicants. Individuals demand that, while they may make their own ethical decisions, the organizations that represent them or offer services to them must have tighter ethical controls and represent their own feelings much more closely. People cannot be dictated to, and with the influence of religion and government waning, individuals take more responsibility for their own lifestyles and decisions. They demand that their employers do the same.

The dark side of corporate social responsibility

CSR is at best enlightened self-interest and at worst cynical corporate spin. All too often CSR programmes consist of sporadic donations to favoured national charities, and are dreamed up by dinosaurs of the capitalist era in a strained attempt to readjust to a new economy and the new demands of its stakeholders. The glossy CSR portfolio at Enron provides a clear example. The energy trader was extremely generous in its donations to good causes in Houston for many years before it transpired that these were merely efforts to 'buy' reputation. This was clearly one example of corporate social dysfunctionality. There is a difference between truly socially involved corporate citizens and those who pay lip service to the notion. When over £8 billion a year is lost by businesses through energy inefficiency, do we really believe that corporate drives to save energy are a purely altruistic move aimed at saving the planet? Are supermarkets really embracing CSR when they develop excellent customer- and employee-focused policies while simultaneously squeezing producers and preventing diversity of production?[48] Consumer cynicism of purported altruism is fuelled when tobacco companies devote many pages of their websites to trumpeting their CSR prowess. We are reaching a point where CSR has become so mercantile that it is losing its real meaning.

A MORI Millennium survey based on 25 000 adults in 23 countries revealed that 56 per cent of respondents felt that corporate responsibility (employee treatment, community commitment, ethics, environment) was an important factor in terms of forming an impression of a company. Yet, 35 per cent of European CEOs (the highest in any region) still see CSR as largely a public relations issue, which is confirmed by the fact that the lowest formal reporting of CSR is in Europe.

There are many examples of CSR masquerading as a social insurance policy or cheap public relations (PR), a mask for deeper problems which then go undetected. This is dysfunctional. Companies are trying to reconcile two conflicting pressures: to cut costs to adjust to tighter margins, and to appeal to an ever-widening circle of stakeholders. Any CSR programme must be credible. That it is certain types of company in particular – tobacco giants, petroleum companies and multinationals – that are so vociferous in portraying themselves as socially responsible is telling. Today's consumers and co-members are much more aware.

The danger with CSR is that it becomes a form of reactionary management, where companies implement policies on the hoof in response to criticism. This must be avoided by formulating a strategy up front. Companies have to get it right: a search on the internet under 'corporate responsibility' reveals a glut of websites dedicated to exposing the unscrupulous organizations whose social responsibility record leaves something to be desired. There are countless examples of companies that have highly publicized CSR policies, but who sack whistle-blowers, lose discrimination suits or have poor diversity records. Accountability and taking responsibility are definite components of a CSR-focused organization.

CSR is about reputation and corporate direction, two key elements that should be reflected and propagated in the corporate badge. Strategic CSR is about living that badge. When part of the wider strategy, CSR stimulates sounder business practices that can deliver bottom-line benefits. In selection by both consumers and employees, a strong commitment to a strategic CSR can provide vital comparative differentiation.

Strategic CSR will impact on all aspects of the organization. It will regulate the business processes. It will affect which markets a company targets, and it will be the founding principle of the HR ethos. The nucleus of the concept is how companies make their profits, not how much they skim off the top to throw at a particular charity. Corporate culture is an excellent indicator of arrogance. The closed, hierarchical and directive cultures of the dinosaurs of capitalism will fail to be successful in the people economy, as talented individuals will choose to direct their skills elsewhere.

A case in point: Happy Computers

Happy Computers, an IT training company based in east London, was founded by Henry Stewart in 1990. He set out to create an environment and a company in which work is a positive experience.

Henry Stewart had experience of entrepreneurial ventures before starting up the company. His first attempt, however, ended in the failure of the left-wing newspaper the *News on Sunday*, which folded after a matter of weeks despite employing a workforce brimming with bright ideas and creativity. The reason: poor management which resulted in an ultimately destructive culture.

At Happy Computers, effective management means open management. For instance, the company practises open book management (OBM), a technique made popular by Richard Semler of Brazilian company Semco. OBM means that every member of staff has access to information on the company's inner financial workings, including salaries. This policy comes into its own when business conditions are difficult, as they generally have been in the IT training industry during 2001 and 2002. Opening up the books empowers the employees; when things get tough they are not reliant solely on managers telling them that times are hard but are able to see for themselves the problems facing the company. The policy stimulates every employee to be concerned about the organization's health, and has changed problem solving from a purely managerial role into an activity that involves the wider workforce.

Happy Computers' social activity is governed by the concept of mutual benefit, the idea that any social or community work carried out must bring benefit not only to the recipient but also to the individual and company. Employees are thus presented with the opportunity to become involved in projects that will contribute to their personal development. For example, in February 2002, two Happy Computers' trainers flew to Kampala, where they worked for a month in a community centre that had received computers from Action Aid. They trained local people in software and training skills, leaving them able to deliver a high standard of education to local people. This project enabled a local IT training infrastructure to be developed and demonstrably enhanced the teaching skills of the two participants.

The company operates a time bank from which staff can apply to carry out concerted programmes with charities that involve work similar to their job. In total, there are 100 volunteer days to draw from, and an employee population of 44. The criteria used to assess the suitability of potential projects is based on the social impact that the work will have, an evaluation of the actual need of the recipient and the mutual benefit anticipated.

Happy Computers' culture is defined by the management's approach to staff empowerment and personal development. This is manifest in numerous practices. The first is the company's volunteering scheme. The company is also happy to accommodate flexible working arrangements. Henry Stewart believes that the onus in areas such as flexible working arrangements should be on companies to demonstrate that ideas could not work as opposed to individuals being obliged to prove that they can. The company is firmly against the long-hours culture that is prevalent within the industry. Even Henry consciously works less hours today than when he founded the company, allowing others to take up some of the slack.

The company's unique culture is maintained by a recruitment policy based on selecting people with an attitude that is congruous with the company's ethics. Undoubtedly, the majority of applicants are attracted by the company's ethical backbone and open culture, which enables the company to differentiate itself as an employer of choice in an industry where competition for talent is fierce. All employees have equality of opportunity to rise through the ranks, some starting in administrative positions before moving more into the training side of the business, with no barriers being placed on personal development. The commitment instilled in the workforce is tangible, with a staff turnover rate of just 5.5 per cent, compared with an industry average of 16 per cent.

In the past, largely because of its social focus, the company generated the majority of its revenue from clients in the public, charity and not-for-profit sectors. This figure was as high as 85 per cent, but since 2000 has been reduced to around 60 per cent. The company's focus on quality is therefore winning it new business from the private sector.

There is no in-house sales or marketing team. In fact, Happy Computers has only ever released one marketing mailshot in over 10 years of delivering training. The company relies exclusively on word-of-mouth advertising, something that necessitates a focus on quality. To ensure that the quality of the company's training is maintained to the highest possible standard, the company is focused on receiving as much feedback as possible. The latest idea of 'once-removed' feedback involves canvassing the clients and commercial partners of the companies who send delegates on training programmes to discern how the training delivered has affected them.

A case in point: The Furniture Resource Centre Group (FRCG)

(This case study is discussed further in Chapter 6.) The Furniture Resource Centre Group's focus on product and co-members actively prevents this successful company slipping into any corporate arrogance. As with any company operating on a for-profit basis, the quality of product and customer service are pivotal to success, and maintaining standards and retaining customers are the two main priorities. In October 2000, the company's management began asking all of its local authority and registered social landlord customers to give them marks out of 10 on their furnishing service. Since then, they have consistently hit the 8-out-of-10 benchmark they set themselves, and send a manager on a personal visit to any customer that gives marks below the benchmark, to find out how service can be improved.

The group has a clear focus on staff development, both personal and professional. Indeed, development is seen very much as an end in itself. FRCG has already trained over 200 long-term unemployed people, facilitating 180 of them to go on to permanent jobs, both inside the company and elsewhere. There has been an increasing emphasis over recent years on self-development and skills such as creativity. Creativity is one of four values (the others being passion, bravery and professionalism) that form the basis of an annual award ceremony. The whole company votes on the individuals believed to have demonstrated the most concrete examples of each value. Line managers are also encouraged to reward particular instances of creativity with instant cash rewards. The next move forward will see the company distribute up to one-third of its bonus kitty in line with how well each individual is perceived to have acted in accordance with the company's values.

Each worker is actively encouraged to seek personal growth through the 'University of the People' an idea based on a similar programme run at South West Airlines in the USA. FRCG's university was set up in January 2002, with three key aims:

■ to provide some form of learning for every member of staff

■ to increase dramatically learning and innovation throughout the FRCG

■ to enable the company to become more successful in achieving its social and economic aims.

The university has three principal development programmes under the generic name Alchemy:

■ Alchemy Gold: a work and development programme for the previously long-term unemployed. The programme includes basic training and development work on professional and personal skills along with job-searching techniques.

■ Alchemy Platinum: the central university programme for everyone, including permanent staff, Alchemy Gold participants and even board members. Each participant learns about career and general life development, communication, marketing and basic IT, among other areas.

■ Alchemy Titanium: an intensive, real-life innovation and development course for the FRCG's brightest potential social entrepreneurs. This is a mixture of formal learning and residential events. All senior managers are automatically members of Alchemy Titanium, and other employees can apply to join it. All each applicant has to do is write a synopsis of why they are suitable for the training; the methods of doing this vary, with some using the traditional approach of writing the answer, others using art or poetry.

Fifty-five members of staff have already attended at least one course through the university, and the company's management seeks to develop an increasing number of courses designed to meet both professional and personal development needs, through a series of 'How's it Going' reviews with senior management and mentors. The workforce can also highlight aspects of their own development through an intracompany body called the Human Resources Advisory Group. This is a group of people elected from different teams across the company.

New co-members are recruited on the basis of attitude not aptitude, a policy designed to retain the company's central spirit as it grows. This attitude is demonstrated by a recruitment game known as 'My Special Thing', in which applicants are asked to sell something close to their heart to an audience of current managers. Meanwhile, effort is made to link different business units together in order to maintain the group's central ethos, achieved in part through the 'Walk a Mile' initiative which sees managers spending time in a different business division every 6 months.

Social businesses like the FRCG teach traditional private-sector companies a lot about the changing nature of business, and are able to demonstrate that the links that bind value chains need not be based solely on cost, but on other values as well. Overall, FRCG is proof positive that characteristics such as social focus will increasingly act as a source of differentiation from your competitors, and can help to prevent any arrogance in success.

Stop, look, listen (and react)

To avoid arrogance, companies should press for negative feedback from clients and actively solicit constructive criticism from co-members. Bland feedback forms provide little assistance, but explicit requests for frustrating or negative aspects of a deal could provide useful information. Customers are good at voicing their frustrations; it used to be frustrating for customers not able to use a credit card at Marks & Spencer and it was frustrating in the past for consumers to be unable to shop at John Lewis on Mondays. Perhaps if these companies had listened to the complaints of their customers sooner, rather than being arrogant in their success, they would not have had to endure the hardships of recent years.

A case in point: NuPrint Trimmings

NuPrint Trimmings, based in Belfast, is a manufacturer of clothing labels for major retailers such as Marks & Spencer. It has engineered a dramatic turnaround in its business fortunes, primarily through an increased commitment to its workforce. In the late 1990s, the company's management took its eye off the changing nature of an industry in which a growing number of operators around the world had started to compete, and as a consequence went into dramatic decline. Yet with a change of management personnel, an increased focus on internal communication of business objectives and enhanced workforce involvement, the company is back on track and expanding rapidly.

The company had enjoyed success from its inception, servicing a predominantly local client base, but this came to a rapid end in the late 1990s. Profits sank dramatically as a result of management failing to keep up with changing realities, a low level of skills among the workforce and a lack of international focus. Consequently, NuPrint suffered a significant financial loss in 1998 and suffered the pullout of its largest customer in 2000.

Today the company is once more thriving. The man behind the company's turnaround in fortunes is MD Gavin Killeen. The fundamental factor underpinning his management focus has been the development of the company's co-members. His success has been swift, with NuPrint expanding by 60 per cent over 3 years and generating a significant amount of international business, despite fiercely competitive trading conditions for the industry as a whole.

Change began with an initial cost-cutting programme to release members of staff who were emotionally uncommitted to the change project. Mr Kileen then built a new managerial focus on training those employees who were committed. Training had been an area completely neglected by the management team in the period running up to the company's fall from profitability. One telling indictment of the previous management was the fact that some of the company's employees had never received any formal training despite having worked there for over 10 years. Mr Killeen set about providing a formal structure to the company's training policy, introducing personal development plans and a structure for achieving National Vocational Qualifications (NVQs). Over and above formal qualifications, the culture has changed significantly, with every member of staff currently on one form of training, creating a more business-aware workforce. To strengthen their human resources further, NuPrint joined a Norwesco programme run by the University of Ulster and Letterkenny. The programme was tailored to help the company to embrace innovation and creativity by involving all co-members in the improvement process.

Added to this new focus on developing HR, came a reorganization of the company's business processes. By focusing on remedying the disconnected management practices of the past, and communicating business needs openly to the workforce, each employee became more fully aware of what was expected of them. The process has led to a cultural change and, above all, a greater focus on teamwork. Moreover, moves towards the establishment of more open communication channels between management and staff have fostered a widespread spirit of emotional ownership.

The impact has been tangible, a prime example being a saving of £24 000 on reduced material wastage over a 12-month period, achieved by increasing material usage rates from 75 to 95 per cent. The company has achieved a reduction of 50 per cent in wastage in the manufacturing process, added to a 50 per cent increase in overall productivity levels, and savings of 75 per cent in lead times in the art and design and main office, where many manual processes were eliminated. Customers have picked up on the fact that the company delivers a better service. Since being taken over by new parent company, International Trimmings, NuPrint has been held up as the group's standard bearer for training, notably in the area of IT. Eighty per cent of NuPrint employees are now IT literate, compared with just 10 per cent when the company first ran into trouble.

NuPrint owes its success to the ability of its new management to deliver cultural change and develop the skills base of its workforce. Its investment in training has paid off, and the company is now running more efficiently than at any other time in its history.

The all-controlling power of (some) stakeholders

The corporate story has changed with the demise of capitalism, and an increasing number of players are contributing to the narrative. There is a wide range of fractious groups whose views are increasingly important. The demands of a growing number of stakeholders are challenging for corporations, not least because of the conflict that commonly arises between these different groups. A power line determines where the real control lies; in pure commodity industries the customer holds the power, but in all other industries and companies where creativity can impact on any part of the process, the co-member is the key priority.

In adapting to the power and influence of stakeholders, companies face difficult decisions. Businesses will now succeed or fail on the strength of their people, and they need to attract the best. However, the conflicting realities of needing to pay key co-members well, and retaining consumers who are unwilling to support indulgent margins, can cause difficulties. The dilemma is to pay sufficiently attractive salaries without alienating other stakeholders. Total board-room pay at Tesco rose by over 40 per cent to £13 million between early 2001 and 2002.[49] Philip Green, the major shareholder of high-street retailer BHS, awarded himself a special dividend amounting to £180 million.[50] Even the Government is preparing to pay the biggest public-sector salary on record to attract a new CEO from the private sector to run the troubled Royal Mail Company: at an estimated £500 000 basic salary, it will be over double what the retiring occupant, John Roberts, received.[51]

At the other end of the spectrum, we will witness more strikes as those in the low-paid occupations have no other weapon but to walk out (at the time of going to press this was evident from the actions of firefighters and tube-workers). According to research by the TUC, pay rises for directors have outstripped wage increases for their workers by 3 to 1 since 1995. Top executives at half of all FTSE companies have bonus schemes entitling them to 100 per cent or more of salary through annual share option bonus awards. The fact that over half of Britain's finance directors believe that companies should refuse to pay bonuses to underperforming directors[52] reinforces the realization that many companies feel obligated to award large bonuses to the alienation of other stakeholders. In the USA, CEOs at larger companies earn an average of $10.6 million a year, an astounding 442 per cent increase over the average salary of $2 million in 1990.

Merrill Lynch Investment Managers have announced that they are to boost salaries for fund managers under a radical new compensation scheme aimed at retaining the best people.[53] Even though Merrill's CEO, Peter Gibbs, noted that there were various reasons for the resignations of around 10 per cent of the company's fund managers in 2001, including lifestyle factors and retirement, the only response that the company has made is to boost the pay packets. The problem with using money to motivate people is that this is a currency readily available to competitors.

Rewarding failure

The real stakeholder conflict arises when organizations insist on rewarding failures. The FTSE 100's top 10 highest paid CEOs received £80.6 million between them in the financial year to 2002. Over the same period the stock market fell by 24 per cent. Barclay Knapp, CEO of 'ntl', received a bonus of almost £400 000 in 2001 (more than double the amount he received in the previous year) as the company teetered towards bankruptcy. Sir Christopher Gent, the CEO of Vodafone Group, received a £5 million cash bonus in 2001, and a salary and bonus of £2.4 million in 2002, as Vodafone reported pre-tax losses in excess of £13.5 billion and the company's stock-market value more than halved. Telewest, the struggling cable television company, awarded its senior executives bonuses of £690 000 as the company plummeted in value from £12 billion in 2000 to just £145 million in 2001. Jac Nasser, the ousted boss of Ford who axed car production in Britain and presided over falling shares, received a staggering golden handshake of £12 million. Gerald Corbett received £444 000 on leaving a shambolic Railtrack. Executives at British Petroleum, Marks & Spencer and J Sainsbury's, among others, received payoffs of between

£600 000 and £1 million. In 2002 the CEO of the Instinet Group received a payoff of nearly £3 million, despite the fact that the US-based company has struggled since being floated, with its shares halving in value. Rolls-Royce gave five directors an increase of up to 48 per cent in their packages in 2001, the same year that the company cut 5000 jobs.

This evidence indicates that, whether it is the best of times or the worst of times, companies are having to pay more to get the top people, and those with requisite talents can name their price. The question begging to be answered is whether, with the level of executive incompetence and poor perform-ance, CEOs are really worth the reward?

One solution is to relate pay to performance as much as possible. This can be done through 'value-added' estimates. It is imperative that the business thinking is tightly connected so that the right performance is measured and individuals are not rewarded for the wrong inputs or outputs. All employees are not created equal. Contractual negotiation is key, particularly in regard to payoffs. These should be performance related to preset broad criteria, which must allow for some element of flexibility in acknowledge-ment of the rapidity of market fluctuations. If pay awards are too big, they may work against the long-term growth in sustainable corporate income, since bonuses based on short- or medium-term targets may encourage questionable acquisi-tions or mergers. The aim should therefore be to set up long-term tracker options to give staggered bonuses. This would also have the welcome consequence of changing the current general culture of hit or miss bonuses.

This concurs with an overall change in the rationale of reward systems throughout all levels of the company structure. The importance of measuring inputs has been superseded by an emphasis on outputs. It is not those who work longest or hardest who should be the most handsomely rewarded, but those who work smartest and offer the most added value, although these may often be the same. There has been a significant increase in the percentage of organizations that reward employees for increased profitability, from 57 per cent in 1994 to 69 per cent in 2000.[54] There have also been increases in group incentives, project incentives, and stock options and grants, all of which are related to performance at some level.

According to Watson Wyatt's Human Capital Index, above-average pay and benefits are associated with an increase in company performance. Therefore, the added value generated by above-average pay (for example, the creation of greater employee commitment) more than outweighs the cost of implementing a properly designed remuneration package.

The best performing firms view their reward programmes differently to less well-performing organizations:

- Top firms are more likely to use rewards as tools to engage people in improving business performance.

- These firms make greater efforts than others to communicate their plans and to measure reward plan effectiveness.

- They are more likely than the rest to link rewards to their organizations' business strategies.

Unique strategic positioning

Most successful companies do well because of a simple combination of a clearly defined strategy and excellent market positioning. These two goals are interlinked. The idea behind unique strategic positioning (USP) is to develop commercial strategies that will have a positive impact on an organization as a whole and increase revenues for the core business. By doing so, investment risk will be controlled.

Reed Executive's strategic goals have taken us into the corporate training market. Every quarter we mail 500 000 training programme brochures to companies around the UK. This is in itself an excellent PR exercise for our recruitment business, and meant initially that even if there was a poor response to the courses on offer the exercise was a positive one in terms of building the company's reputation as a multi-service provider. However, the USP of developing a strong training function runs deeper than this. The brochure offers courses at all levels in the fields of management development, human resources, finance, sales, marketing and IT. It informs potential clients and candidates, as well as shareholders and suppliers, that we have expertise in each of these areas. The strategic advantage is that our co-members can attend the course, which improves their skills and career development, which in turn benefits the internal running of the company. In addition, clients can be invited to attend, which is excellent client-relations management and a powerful incentive for client retention. This also results in clients being on the same courses as co-members, providing networking opportunities beneficial to the company, a fourth strategic benefit. By uniquely strategically positioning the company to ensure that Reed Training adds value to the core business of Reed Executive, we have developed a 'win–win–win–win' strategy benefiting co-members, clients, potential customers and the main company.

The thinking is ...

Information and the speed with which it can be disseminated make all companies vulnerable to hostile scrutiny at a time when reputation and badge building are vital to success. Lapsing into the arrogance of success is the quickest way for a company to free-fall into failure. Despite well-meaning and oft-quoted corporate slogans which herald the importance of listening to stakeholders, slipping into arrogance is easily done. Principal indicators of corporate arrogance include a poorly focused remuneration structure where failures are rewarded, and operating a corporate social responsibility programme that has more to do with marketing and public relations than it has about strategy. To avoid corporate arrogance, companies should actively seek specific criticisms from a broad spectrum of stakeholders, and act accordingly. Remuneration should have some aspect of flexibility for added value linked in, and an open culture of respect and development should be nurtured. Lastly, companies must commit resources to the continuous training of all co-members and must ensure that corporate strategy is tightly focused on achieving goals by developing their own unique strategic positionings.

CHAPTER 5

Harnessing the power

There is compelling evidence of a correlation between people management and business performance, a correlation that is both positive and cumulative: the greater the number of effective practices that are used, the better the result.[55] However, the results of surveys in the UK and USA reveal that only 10 per cent of companies prioritize their people over marketing or finance issues.[55] This is exceptionally shortsighted and ill-considered business practice. Human talent is the most important value driver for all companies. A dynamic approach to human resource (HR) management is required. Two principal tasks must be met head-on by business; the first is to develop a combination of HR practices which achieve organizational objectives, and the second is to create a working environment that attracts and satisfies the human talent required.

This chapter will outline solutions to the principal challenges facing business: skill shortages, and how to attract and retain key talent. Strategies on how to recognize, measure and develop one of the most important competencies for competitive advantage, intuitive intelligence, will also be explored.

Skill scarcity

Over 1000 organizations in the UK are regularly surveyed for the Reed Skills Index, which has tracked demand for talent since May 1997. The index reveals that well over half of organizations regularly find it difficult to recruit suitably qualified and experienced staff. In 2000, for the first time, skill shortages were deemed to be the most pressing concern for the FTSE 100 leaders. In the Peoplist Economy this is set to remain a major concern.

Many of the fundamental solutions to the problem of national skills shortages, such as having a more progressive approach to immigration and offering better adult-education provision, can only be invoked by government action. However, companies that have a flexible and open-minded approach can ease their difficulties.

A case in point: Café Spice Namaste

The cosmopolitan hospitality industry includes over 15 000 establishments serving South Asian foods in the UK. The restaurant sector suffers from a high rate of failure, and margins are low. The founder and owner of Café Spice Namaste, Cyrus Todiwala, believes that a commitment to developing and improving skills is the secret to success of his East London chain of Indian restaurants. The company has struggled to find the requisite skills within the local population base. Mr Todiwala took it upon himself to develop these skills, and in doing so has sought to place the personal development of co-members as a key business concern. This approach has brought with it considerable commercial success.

His business philosophy is simple: companies that fail to invest in their people do not invest in themselves. Mr Todiwala has gone to considerable lengths to encourage and accommodate personal development, by supporting employees in career training unrelated to the hospitality industry.

He has set up English language classes to develop the linguistic skills of his co-members. The training is also open to employees working in rival restaurants, reflecting a belief that what is good for the improvement of skills in the industry in general is good for Café Spice in particular.

Another of Mr Todiwala's key concerns is to bring more profession-alism to the industry. Coupled with a desire to facilitate new chefs to be able to learn the traditional skills of Asian cookery and contribute to the generation of new ideas, this has led Mr Todiwala and two partners to set up the country's first ever Asian cookery school, the Asian and Oriental School of Catering. The Academy has provided in-house training for prestigious restaurants such as La Porte des Indes and Cafe Lazeez. In September 2000 the Academy opened its doors and welcomed students onto the Certificate and Diploma in Asian Food Preparation and Cooking. It was announced 'College of the Year' by the London Tourism Board in 2001 for its innovative ways of developing skills.

The genuine commitment to skills development and personal growth has paid dividends. In addition to developing the customer-facing and line-management skills needed to function on a day-to-day business, Mr Todiwala has managed to create a culture of emotional ownership in which individual employees genuinely care about the company and its future development. One employee, who was backed by Café Spice

Namaste to train as a computer systems analyst while working in one of the restaurants and now earns a considerable wage, returns each weekend to Café Spice simply because he feels that he belongs there. This sense of ownership is valuable when business conditions are as competitive as they are in the London restaurant business. It also contributes to the organic growth of the business, with the company basing its desired business diversification firmly on the ideas, skills and ingenuity of its workforce. The commitment and involvement of the workforce have led to a diversification of service, with the company running an internet site on the medicinal benefits of Indian spices.

Axe the average

Ousting average performers is a different issue to the ill-considered cutbacks at times of economic uncertainty that were discussed in Chapter 2. When it comes to terminating the employment of an ineffectual member of staff, HR professionals often lament the fact that their hands are bound by rigorous regulation and legislation. There is a no-man's land that stretches between those who offer clearly defective performance, and can easily be identified, and those actually adding significant value to an organization, and for whom the most pressing organizational concerns are retention issues. The cleverly work-shy are afforded incubation by stringent employment legislation. However, a more creative approach by HR can facilitate the removal of individuals adding no value to an organization, and make room for those with potential.

Probation periods are quite commonly used for new graduates and younger employees, yet broader adoption offers limitless options. By offering a basic salary and a performance bonus, HR gives itself financial leverage from which it is able to have more influence on the tenure of each employee. Upon consistently poor performance, the bonus can be cut or dropped altogether, leaving only the basic salary and a powerful incentive to go. Naturally, the criteria against which the bonus is calculated must be fair and agreed at the start of the contract, and should offer the same benefits and support clauses across the organization. In standardizing its approach, an organization calms any worries that may be felt by an enthusiastic new member and instead instills in the culture the belief that adding value will be rewarded. It is not wise to decide upon an arbitrary figure to axe in Jack Welch style, as this works against the ethos of peoplism. Companies should have in place excellent systems and follow fair procedures to ensure that the right people are identified and nurtured.

Many poor performers slip through the probationary net purely by accident. New recruits whom the company may not necessarily want to keep may be afforded contractual protection by reaching both internal and legislative milestones if the whole probationary process is not well managed. HR can prevent this eventuality by using management information systems that automatically notify line-management before the achievement of these probationary milestones. By taking this proactive approach, the company does not become burdened by these underperforming staff who never quite make the grade. In a similar vein, at Reed we promote internally usually on a

12-month probationary period. We also spread bonuses forward in order to retain talented individuals.

Companies must adopt innovative strategies to be able to attract, recruit and retain enough talented co-members, and to ensure that their potential is fulfilled in terms of the enterprise and creativity they bring to the organization. A business is in the hands of its operators, so it is important to make sure that they are not average.

Holistic HR: the seven stages of work

HR is a strategic component of business success. It is more important than ever to have a fully integrated game plan. To this end, companies must take a holistic approach to HR management. The seven-stage work life cycle comprises attraction, recruitment, induction, career development and training, reward, retention and separation.

It is imperative that the HR function is innovative, progressive and flexible at each stage in order to make a bottom-line impact on the business.

1. Attraction

When it comes to attracting employees, companies need to go and look for them in the places they are likely to find them, rather than relying solely on conventional means of advertising that tend to be less focused on a particular target audience. By developing their own consistent corporate badge, they can look to attract people to their companies who embody their own values.

Employer badges can have a bottom-line impact, firstly on recruitment by minimizing the cost and time per hire as candidates self-select, secondly on retention, by building loyalty, and thirdly on productivity, by driving co-member commitment to the achievement of corporate strategy. The first step is identifying the objectives and goals that you want the employer badge to achieve. Consistency is key, and it must be born of organizational values into which all co-member needs are integrated. This approach ensures that external promises are met and new recruits' expectations are fulfilled. You must target your employee profile to ensure that you get the right badge.

View employees as customers and make a similar effort to attract them. Make as much information available as possible to encourage self-selection. Talented people attract talented people, so encourage key staff to recommend their friends and contacts for positions.

2. Recruitment

An uncertain economy and a shortage of key skills have created a challenging time for recruiters. Recruitment policies need to embrace multifarious networks of contact. Employee referral schemes are a way of capitalizing on the network of contacts that key members already have within the company. 'Talent scouts', who may work for the company on a permanent, part-time or casual basis, can be on the lookout for tomorrow's talent within our schools and education system, or today's talent in other organizations. Companies can look to develop 'feeder' relationships with other companies where each supplies the other with people they feel may be more suited to work for them.

Talent moves at the speed of light, so eradicate all unnecessary delays. More than two-thirds of applicants consider the interview process an accurate indicator of how the company runs, and therefore firms should be aware that a poor process can amount to a public relations disaster. If 50 per cent of your selection is successful, you are doing very well. In particular, companies should measure the attrition rate of graduate recruits.

3. Induction

Induction is a valuable, yet often neglected, necessity for instilling and encouraging a spirit of innovation and enterprise into new employees. First impressions count, and there is no better opportunity to demonstrate a company's innovative approach to HR management. Stimulate creativity in inductees by allowing them to become acclimatized via imaginative exercises. Instead of only throwing leaving parties, throw joining parties to show the value of new co-members from day one. Line managers must take full responsibility for continuing the process of induction for their new staff. Structured coaching and reviewing processes, as well as systems for monthly reviews, 6-monthly appraisals and continuous evaluation of performance and development, should be fitted as standard. Companies must view induction in its full context. Before induction, the recruitment process is all about attracting people with the right talents to do the job. The induction programme itself should be about turning these talents into performance as quickly as possible. After induction, the line manager follow-up should be about enabling the new recruit to apply their talents in the work-place.

4. Career development and training

New generations of workers fresh out of university are far more assertive in their dealings with employers than previous generations were. Increasing numbers of individuals are demanding the right to construct their careers in different ways. In The Netherlands, for example, there is a fast growing trend for professionals to seek to work 4-day weeks. In the UK, mid-career breaks, often more than one, are becoming popular among a workforce that sees more to life than work. These employees look for more in their employers than purely financial reward, and issues such as companies' social action and ethical foundation are increasingly becoming a source of differentiation in employer brands.

The psychological contract between worker and employer has broken down in many industries as a result of past recessions and corporate restructuring, to the extent that loyalty is fast diminishing. Talented individuals are loyal only to the company that matches their own personal development goals. Employees, in short, have become consumers of careers. Maintain the enthusiasm generated at induction through supportive career development and training programmes. Learning is now seen as a lifelong process, and a commitment to personal development is the cornerstone of the new psychological contract between employer and employee. Of top priority is that employees need to develop the ability to 'learn how to learn quickly'. Encourage cross-functionality and cross-fertilization of knowledge by providing employees with learning opportunities with both intradepartmental and interdepartmental secondments: it should not only be the CEO who has a 'helicopter view' of the company. Encourage fluidity of movement within the company and make functional boundaries more permeable: it is eminently less costly, after all, to 'retain and retrain' than to 'fire and rehire' when filling a position. Give staff control over their training needs and reward them for taking it.

5. Reward

Capitalist reward structures shone on those who used the resources at their disposal to develop more capital, traditionally rewarding individuals in proportion to the amount of profit they created. The reward priorities were to shareholders and those who discernibly added financial value, such as business developers or client managers.

This hierarchy has changed in the peoplist economy. Co-members are more important than capital, and the focus of reward structures should readjust in favour of those who develop people as much as those who develop capital. In the peoplist economy the individual who recruits key members to the organization is as important as the business development manager. The person (whether they are based in HR or in any other division) who invests time in individuals by coaching and developing those people is the peoplist client manager.

An excellent example of a peoplist reward strategy designed to garner commitment comes from Jim Chain, the owner of an engineering company based in the mid-West of America. His company outlines the job duties and allows employees to develop their own job description and determine (with the help of an adviser) how they will evaluate their own progress. The initial stages of the programme act to separate those who can work on their own from those who require supervision. The reward system is then designed to involve everyone sharing the profit, based upon their individual commitment to the company.

6. Retention

In all of the stages of the HR life cycle it is important that HR departments look to individualize their strategies and policies in order to meet the needs of their key co-members. Money is still, and is likely to remain, the major motivator in the field of employee reward. However, individualism has supplanted materialism as the driving force in many people's lives, and employees increasingly have aspirations over and above the accumulation of personal wealth. People now want to accumulate 'life experience', or concentrate more on relationships outside the work context: they want to attain their own ideal of work–life balance. If there is one central philosophy that underpins this new approach to employee reward it is that HR managers should look to reward employees in the way in which they want to be rewarded: it should be as much a bottom–up as a top–down process.

Individuals no longer ask, 'Why should I leave?' but 'Why should I stay?' Companies need to create a wall of opportunities to retain key staff.

Offer sabbaticals to employees whom you want to keep but who may wish to take career breaks. Look for contractual tie-ins. What can you offer your key employees to cement their attachment to your company? Can you help those with children by providing babycare facilities? Can you help those with care responsibilities for elderly relatives by providing a 'granny crèche'? Some local authorities are offering teachers accommodation as part of their remunerative packages. Could this principle be extended to the private sector, and the old principle of 'tied houses' be given a modern update? Buddy different levels of staff, for networking, cross-fertilization and support purposes.

7. Separation

When separation occurs, after all it is inevitable in the modern workplace, employers should maintain their relationship with ex-employees. Each former employee is, after all, released into the world as a walking, talking, word-of-mouth advertisement for the company. University-style 'alumni' relationships are a good way of maintaining contact with people who may prove valuable for the company in the future. KPMG, which has an average staff turnover of 20 per cent launched an alumni programme in 1992 with 7000 members, and is now in touch with 18000 alumni throughout the UK. There is always the chance that these former employees will come back into the company. It is important to draw up ground rules as to what can and cannot be networked.

As mentioned in Chapter 2, there must be an HR strategy for dealing with economic ebbs and flows: firing and rehiring are simply not viable; they are expensive both financially and in terms of motivation, and companies should demonstrate greater flexibility and adaptability in dealing with these circumstances. Get managers to commit to the value of key workers before they leave. Divide work into projects so that, in an economic slowdown, projects are cut, not talent.

A case in point: Charlton Athletic Football Club

In the world of professional football the onus on securing the best talent, be it coach or player, is particularly acute. Ultimately, it is the job of the manager to bring the on-field success that forms the basis of the club's financial performance.

Charlton is managed by Alan Curbishley, who has now been in charge for over 10 years, and is regarded as one of the most talented young coaches in the UK. In his time at the club he has achieved considerable success, first by winning promotion to the Premier League and more recently by consolidating the club's position in the top flight. Larger clubs have been interested in appointing him, yet Alan Curbishley remains Charlton's manager and a key part of its talent infrastructure.

The liquidity of the football industry, particularly at the top level, has changed dramatically over recent years. With the influx of massive amounts of money resulting from lucrative television deals conducted between the Premier League and BSkyB, there has been a dramatic spiralling of player wages and transfer fees. David

Beckham, although not the country's highest paid player, is rumoured to receive £70 000 per week in basic wages plus £20 000 a week in image rights. In 1997, Charlton's record signing was Clive Mendonca, whose transfer fee of £700 000 appeared small change compared to the combined £7.5 million that the club spent on just two players, Jason Euell and Luke Young, before the start of the 2001–02 season. The club now has a core of international-class players that helped secure ninth place in the Premiership table in May 2001, a level of success that even the club's management admits was beyond its expectations in 1997 when the club was in the First Division and in financial difficulty.

However, such talent does not come cheap and the club's spending on wages rose from £2.2 million in 1997 to over £14 million in 2002, a staggering rate of inflation, and a liability that must be met by increasing commercial income by the same rate. In total, the club invested over £20 million in the year between the summer breaks of 2000 and 2001. One area in which the club is committed to balancing this situation is investment in its youth development scheme: £1.5 million of capital expenditure relating to the youth academy is ample demonstration of the club's commitment.

Developing the business

To sustain the player investment that brings success on the field, football clubs must increasingly look to new avenues to increase their revenue. Charlton has been innovative and open minded in its approach to creating new revenue streams, a philosophy that comes right from the top in the form of CEO Peter Varney, who has a background in fundraising for charity. The club's approach to developing its business has been highly successful without mortgaging its future under a mountain of debt.

Things were very different in the late 1980s. Despite achieving promotion to the then First Division in 1984, the financial condition of the club deteriorated to such an extent that the former Charlton Athletic Football Company Ltd was wound up in 1984. The club was also forced to vacate its home, The Valley, after which the team played home fixtures as paying tenants at Crystal Palace, but by doing so largely alienated itself from a generation of local fans. By 1996, the club had returned to The Valley, but only to a stadium with a capacity of 15 000 and average attendance of just over 11 000. During 1996 turnover was just under the £3 million mark, and the club made an operating loss before transfers of over £700 000.

The turnaround in the club's financial fortunes since then has been dramatic. Part of the reason for this is its sound financial management. Whereas other clubs budget for high predicted finishes in the league with correspondingly higher revenues, Charlton works on a 'worst case scenario' basis. Annual budgets, the biggest outlay of which is on player wages, are calculated on the assumption that the club will finish 17th in the Premier League, one place above the relegation zone. This has obvious implications for assumed revenue for the year, with income steadily increasing the higher a club finishes, owing to involvement in more televised games and actual prize money. Some clubs budget to finish higher than they actually do to facilitate more spending on players, but this is not the sort of optimistic accounting that sits well with Charlton's focus on prudent management and long-term decision making. With the advent of the new 3 year television agreement with BSkyB in 2001 which brought with it an increased level of revenue to the Premier

League, numerous other clubs took on high levels of long-term debt ranging in value from £20 million to 80 million. In some of these financial arrangements, clubs are using their future revenues to underpin current spending, and not looking to the future, which may involve relegation, making many of the commitments in terms of player contracts unsustainable.

Charlton is continually looking for innovative new ways of growing its business. It currently has a database totalling 45 000 customers with an attachment to Charlton, all of whom hold potential value to the club. It is crucially important to convert those with an interest in the club into regular supporters and customers, and at the same time grow the fan base.

In many respects, the marketing opportunities afforded to clubs operating in the Premier League such as Charlton are unique. Premiership Football is a product consumed in 140 countries around the world. Charlton has been quick to recognize its branding potential in this international market and reach out to new fans. For example, pre-season tours are now run so that football and commercial operations run side by side. The very location of these tours is determined to develop new business opportunities and introduce the club to receptive markets. Scandinavia has been a popular destination for Charlton as a means of developing the already established fan base there.

In an attempt to develop its international brand awareness, Charlton has recognized the value of attaching itself to the support of other countries' national football heroes. Charlton promotes domestic players in the country they are visiting, with the aim of gradually increasing awareness of Charlton as a brand in its own right, independent of the player. The branding exercise is backed up by the production of merchandise branded specifically with national flags and players' names. The next step in the cultivation of these new groups of supporters is own language content on the club's website, and other services specifically tailored to their needs.

Customer closeness: Charlton in the community

As the result of the lost generation of fans that the club suffered during the dark days of its ground-sharing arrangement with Crystal Palace, the club has made it a priority to develop deep roots within the local community, its natural constituency for fans.

The club is clearly focused on the need to communicate effectively with its supporters. Over 5000 supporters receive a daily email bulletin providing them with news on the clubs activities as well as merchandising offers.

Charlton also plays an extremely active role in the local community, operating one of the country's largest and most successful Football in the Community schemes, which reaches over 56 000 schoolchildren each year through their award-winning coaching initiatives.

Charlton is adept at customer retention and looks for long-term relationships with customers. Diversification in product offering includes lifelong season tickets and a 5-year VIP scheme. Over 800 supporters have already taken the opportunity to show their commitment to the club by purchasing 5-year season tickets. Together, these schemes have generated in the order of £1.6 million for the club.

At home, Charlton is aiming to grow two of its core business operations, in the fields of catering and printing. Charlton's commercial management is keen to establish The Valley as a 7-day-a-week business operation, and the latest accounts saw off-the-field revenues increase by 25 per cent. One way in which Charlton is looking to develop its business activities is through farming the emotional ties that link supporters to the club. Supporters have control of large amounts of personal and corporate spend, spend that could be increasingly directed towards the club.

The club's success in increasing its operating revenue has allowed for a higher level of investment in the team. Over recent years, the club has brought in a number of international stars, who bring with them their own fan base and increase the commercial merchandising opportunities for the club.

To increase its exposure in London, Charlton has initiated a series of marketing campaigns in partnership with Capital Radio. It has instigated an aggressive, targeted pricing policy based on cheap tickets to attract families. A season ticket behind the goal at Charlton costs £235, cheaper than tickets at second division Gillingham. By following this tribal, targeted customer approach, the club has ensured high attendance figures at home games, with an average of 26 000 fans attending in the latter half of the 2001–02 season. The number of fans holding a season ticket rose from 5500 in 1997 to almost 22 500 in 2002.

Charlton Athletic is a success story in an overtly peoplist industry. Much of this success stems from its attempts to develop deep roots in the local community and develop an increasing closeness with its supporter network. The club faces an industry in which the human talent it utilizes becomes increasingly expensive year on year, but has succeeded in increasing off-the field revenue to match. The club's innovative approach to developing its business bodes well for its future at a time when clubs exhibiting the static business practices of the past will increasingly struggle for survival.

Boosting the corporate libido

In as many areas as possible, organizations should aim to cultivate an 'X-factor' to encourage innovation, enterprise and creativity. The most profitable way to do this is through constant innovation in business processes and practices. Successful innovation in business is not a series of inventions or breakthroughs, but the consistent improvement of business processes, products and human resource structures. Companies must develop a 'gene pool' of complementary talents to this end.

Across 22 countries, almost 70 per cent of executives think their employees lack the entrepreneurial spirit.[56] Yet there is also evidence that while companies want their employees to be more enterprising, they do not trust them to be, nor do they have the structures in place (or indeed the lack of them) to facilitate innovative and enterprising behaviours. A survey showed that only 16 per cent of companies have a strategy in place for promoting innovation and 25 per cent address innovation in an ad hoc way.[57]

Creativity cannot be slotted into traditional office spaces and working hours, so new ways of working are key. Employees need to have the space, empowerment, support and collaborative resources to be enterprising. It is important that innovative ideas are encouraged to materialize. This can be done through simulation to try out innovative concepts, and by devising performance measures, which should be part of the management structure. Brainstorming, cross-team working, a no-blame culture, strong and open communication avenues, corporate attitude and consulting customers about future needs are key. Make sure it is not just managers who are expected to be innovative.

A case in point: Clearwater

Although only 3 years old, Clearwater, in Bradford, has a turnover of almost £3 million and employs 23 people. The company has revolutionized bath making, applying the engineering skills of the company's owners to an industry in which manufacturers must constantly strive to differentiate their products.

Innovation is at the heart of the company's activity, and although competitors are certainly able to copy Clearwater's new products soon after they arrive on the market, these companies lack the ability to innovate themselves. This allows Clearwater to guide the market in its preferred direction.

Clearwater brings out a new product every 5 weeks, and has concept-to-production time of only 3 weeks, far superior to the industry standard of 2 years. The key to this is staff flexibility. All co-members are trained in each of the five major skill areas required in the bath production process: mould-making, laminating, vacuum forming, chop-spraying and finishing. Added to this, the company makes all of its own tools for each job, enhancing flexibility especially when things do not go to plan and changes are made to the process, which require new tools to be developed.

As a result, Clearwater has become an industry leader in a very short space of time and has won national awards for its enterprising business practices. One of the reasons that the company is so agile in its product development is the culture of positive thinking that the management has sought to develop. Indeed, a positive can-do attitude is the first thing the team looks for when recruiting new employees.

Another way to boost the corporate libido is to actively promote diversity in the workplace. Companies in the past have been keen to tailor their recruitment strategies to ensure that new employees will fit in with clearly defined concepts of their own corporate image. The resultant pool of staff has consequently had a tendency to be homogeneous, with outlooks and approaches in keeping with that of the company, and with each other. Companies have had a tendency to crush individual creativity and innovation to ensure that everyone 'sang from the same hymnsheet'. Now the balance of power has been reversed, with organizations bending over backwards to accommodate the unique skills of talented individuals.

A manifestation of this trend is that many companies have come to question the regimentation of their former recruitment strategies, and are now looking to create a more diverse workforce. By looking beyond the notion of the conventional 'archetypal' employee, companies can not only avoid falling foul of present and future anti-discriminatory legislation, but also create a more diverse and innovative workforce. Taking on a quota of 'wild-card' appointments (i.e. people who do not necessarily come equipped with the conventional skills and/or experience for a role) is one way of doing this.

Diversity can provide a vital boost. Talented workers from a variety of backgrounds can produce creative abrasion. Two different perspectives clash and recombine to produce new solutions to old problems; thesis and antithesis producing synthesis. Hiring people from different backgrounds gives companies an insight into different groups within our multi-cultural society. Hiring people of different ages, genders and backgrounds means that problems are tackled from a range of different angles, and with more relevance to the consumer base of most companies.

In 2001, 13 per cent of graduates in the UK were from ethnic minorities and 52 per cent were female. The market-place is a global one, and companies need a diverse make-up of staff to reflect this. The UK is enjoying an influx of foreign professionals. In 1998, 16 per cent of public limited company directors in the FTSE 150 were from overseas; by 2001 the figure was 23 per cent,[58] partly owing to the reduced supply of homegrown talent and partly owing to a desire to reflect the global nature of most businesses. 'British' companies such as Lloyds TSB, Barclays, Marks & Spencer, Safeway, Selfridges, Burberry, Pearson, British Airways and Pilkington now all have a non-British head, reinforcing the fact that talented individuals can travel anywhere they wish. One of our major assets is the appeal of London and the UK: we had better ensure it remains a good place to work in the future.

Intuitive intelligence: a must-have

Intuition describes the process that occurs when a judgement is made or a decision reached without method or procedure.

An intuitive co-member may often be unable to articulate the precise aspects of a given situation to which he or she is responding. Intuitive thinking is typically rapid, based on subconscious processes, and is most likely to be used in novel situations when only incomplete information is available. Intuitive and rational processes are not mutually incompatible, and the most effective decision makers are typically excellent at both intuitive and rational thinking.

Conditions where key decision makers have only fragmented knowledge, or when a rapid decision is needed, proliferate in dynamic environments, making intuitive decision making essential for business success.

Components of intuitive intelligence

Research carried out by Michael Eysenck, Professor of Psychology at Royal Holloway University of London, analysed the constituent elements of intuitive intelligence. He suggests that there are four components in total, two of which refer to thinking or intellectual abilities and two of which refer to preferences or personality styles:

- the ability to perform intellectual functions requiring little learning or formal instruction

- the ability to think rapidly and decisively without needing to have recourse to logical modes of thinking

- a clear preparedness to contemplate the unknown and to use unconventional approaches; to be independent and original in one's thinking

■ a high level of self-confidence, especially in the value of one's intuitive ideas.

Overall, effective individuals with high levels of intuitive intelligence have excellent intellectual machinery, rapid and decisive non-logical thought processes, high motivation to think intuitively, and the courage of their convictions. This last quality is essential. Those proposing decisions on the basis of intuition cannot support their position with detailed factual evidence, and so generally have to rely on their personal powers of persuasion or power base. In addition, individuals who have low self-confidence generally suffer from anxiety, an emotional state that has an adverse effect on intuitive thinking.

Effective intuitive intelligence requires the presence of all four components. Someone lacking only the ability to think rapidly and decisively would be at a serious disadvantage in situations in which it is essential to respond rapidly to a changing environment. Someone with high intellectual ability, rapid thought processes and high self-confidence, but lacking a willingness to think in unconventional and original ways would be excellent at rational thinking, but would be very poor at thinking outside their comfort zone. Finally, someone who had high intellectual ability, rapid thought processes, and a preference for thinking in original and unconventional ways, but who lacked confidence in their ideas, would be good at intuitive thinking, but would be unduly cautious about pushing their own ideas to influence decision making.

Measuring intuitive intelligence

Each of these four components can be assessed in an organizational context.

Intelligence

There is a fundamental division of intelligence into crystallized and fluid intelligence. Crystallized intelligence depends to a large extent on the knowledge an individual has accumulated during his or her lifetime, and is assessed by tests of general information, arithmetic, spelling and vocabulary. By contrast, fluid intelligence involves the ability to simplify complex relationships and to solve problems in the absence of substantial relevant learning. It is assessed by various tests such as block designs, reasoning and spatial visualization. Fluid intelligence is the type of intelligence that is of direct relevance to intuitive intelligence and which will confer greatest competitive advantage in the people economy.

Rapid, non-logical thinking

This could be assessed by using tests in which people are presented with complex information and must decide on an appropriate answer so rapidly that they cannot make use of logical thought processes. It would be possible to use two equivalent tests, one of which is completed at high speed and one of which is completed much more slowly. Those with effective rapid non-logical thinking would show less of a discrepancy between performance on those two tests than other people.

Motivation for intuitive thinking

What is most relevant here is an emphasis on approaches to decision making. A measure to assess a willingness to reach decisions rapidly in the absence of clear and detailed information is needed. There is a clear overlap here with the Myers–Briggs preference for being a perceptive type, which is in turn related to impulsiveness. The Myers–Briggs Type Indicator is a self-report personality inventory designed to give individuals information about their psychological type. A suitable psychometric test here would combine elements of the intuitive and perceptive types from the Myers–Briggs, but would be refocused to consider decision-making preferences.

Self-confidence

There are two aspects that need to be assessed here. Firstly, we are concerned with self-confidence in the sense of believing strongly in the correctness of one's own thinking and decision-making processes, rather than with self-confidence in social situations. Secondly, there is an emotional aspect to self-confidence, in that individuals who are high in self-confidence typically have low levels of anxiety and depression. It would be relatively straightforward to devise a psychometric questionnaire to assess these two aspects of self-confidence.

Invest in your own 'investors in people' programme

At best, companies can hope to harness the power of talented individuals for a limited time. One way in which they can extend this period for graduate recruits is to 'invest in their people', literally. In the UK, a typical graduate in 2002 will enter the workplace with over £9000 of student debt. Companies can retain enthusiastic and talented graduates by investing in them, and in the process ease their financial burden. The scheme works like this: the individual remains the principal shareholder in their career, and their employing company negotiates a stake by paying off part, or all, of their debt. The repayments from talented individuals can be determined by any number of criteria, including deductions from salary, value-adding performance, the number of innovative ideas submitted, involvement in successful projects and so on. The financial outlay for the company is not too major, and such a gesture inspires commitment from the graduate. The investment is also more prudent than an extravagant 'golden hello' because it illustrates to the new co-member the ways in which they can add value to the company, and to themselves. It starts the relationship off positively and shows the level to which the company has a stake in the development of each talented co-member.

Stretching the fabric: maximizing resources

Work to go

Research drawn up by the Government shows that the main obstacle to cutting excessive working hours is a reluctance by top managers to award the flexibility they did not receive when working their way up the ladder. More than one in five full-time male employees and one in six female employees work more than 48 hours a week in the UK. The fact is that younger employees will increasingly choose companies according to the level of flexibility they are willing to offer.

The industrial revolution brought with it the first commuters, as workers left home-based production and local farms to travel to town-centralized factories. In part, the technological and peoplist age is slowly reversing this movement, facilitating the relocation of the workplace to more convenient pastures. Since 1992 the average distance travelled to work has risen from 11.5 to 13.4 km.[59] We travel over 2600 km a year either commuting or on business in the UK.[60] There is evidence that people have become more willing to travel in short bursts rather than relocate in an era of job insecurity. Although gradual, the rise of teleworking reverses the trend of commuting which came about with the industrial revolution and the birth of the dislocated workplace. In 2001, 2.2 million people in the UK – 7.4 per cent of the employed population – were 'teleworkers' for a significant part of their working week. This represents an increase of 65 per cent on the 1997 figure. Most research shows that people who are out of the office work harder than those behind their desks.

Flexible working is one of the most effective methods of chipping away at a staid and inflexible organizational culture. The growth in part-time work and the increasing professionalism of the workplace are fundamental shifts. Between 1999 and 2010, 2 million jobs will be added to the economy. Two-thirds of these are expected to be taken by women, while the majority will be part-time.[61]

Flexible working should not just be employer driven, but employer and employee driven. It is important that other members of an organization are trained up so that if individuals request a more flexible arrangement, that request can be accommodated.

A case in point: Dutton Engineering

Dutton is a host company for the Department of Trade and Industry's 'Inside UK Enterprise' national scheme, sharing best practice ideas with businesses all over the UK and overseas. It has been awarded best small to medium-sized enterprise (SME) in the UK. The company is currently growing by 20 per cent per annum and has a turnover approaching £3.5 million.

Over its 30-year history, Dutton has always seen its workforce as the key to its success, and the management team has taken the view that while new technologies can be bought and business processes modernized, corporate culture cannot easily be replicated. The company has developed a culture in which co-members are genuinely empowered to contribute to the successful running of the company. All employees have become self-inspecting as individuals and as self-managed teams, and the company has dispensed with a central inspection unit. Teams are not allowed to grow beyond 12 people, the number at which the company believes bonds of communication and innovative working are lost.

Creativity plays its part. Co-members, when empowered by the kind of open culture that Dutton has developed, are eager to try out new things. Dutton's management does not ask for ideas to be sent in for consideration, instead it suggests that co-members attempt to implement ideas first to see if they succeed in the workplace. This is true empowerment and has brought with it tangible success, lead times in one product area group having been reduced from 3 weeks to a little over 8 hours. In addition, each product team has been given direct responsibility for its customer relationships, a move that has brought the company closer to its clients.

Quality control

Thorough appraisals can be the key to superior performance. American management consultancy McKinsey & Company uses appraisals to eliminate what they call the 'C players', thereby relieving the company of the costs of underperformance. Blanket praise helps neither the individual nor the company. What is needed are critical approvals. Because of the increased importance of teamwork, they should no longer be hierarchical, top–down affairs. If the aim is to make systematic improvements in performance, strategy must be translated into specific team and individual goals, which can be measured and accounted for in appraisals, isolating the necessary skills development and mentoring opportunities. An integrated approach is required. There should be some element of 360-degree feedback.

Designer labels

Companies are increasingly giving their staff new high-level and elaborate job titles rather than pay rises. Research by our internet site, reed.co.uk, has identified this new phenomenon, 'uptitling', which is being used by companies across the country to motivate and retain staff when budgets are tight.

More than 1700 workers in the UK were surveyed, with two-thirds of respondents believing that the use of long and higher level job titles ('director', 'head', 'chief') has grown in their organizations since 2000. Large organizations particularly are turning to uptitling, with three-quarters of large firms using this tactic to retain their workforce.

Nearly half of all employees thought a new job title would improve their happiness at work, even if their responsibilities did not change. Workers saw a new job title as a signal that they are valued by their organization and a good career step, raising their profile within the organization. Uptitling is a symptom of a business world where change continues to accelerate. Higher level titles can be seen as a way of empowering people to take responsibility and grasp opportunities as they arise.

The research demonstrates that for many who seek recognition of their contribution to the organization it can be motivational to gain a prestigious job title. It can be especially valuable at a time of economic uncertainty, where resources are tight but the need to retain and incentivize top talent is more important to company success than ever.

A case in point: ?What *If!*

?What *If!*, an innovation and creativity consultancy based in west London, is more than just an employer of creative people: the company markets itself as a way of life. The company was set up in 1992 by a group of friends who had become disillusioned with their careers in traditional multinational consumer goods companies. They felt unable to express their personalities and creative desires within the traditional corporate environment. To this end, the company has engendered a very open culture, demonstrable by the files found on tables in the entrance to the company's headquarters that contain 50 interesting (and in some cases very personal) facts about each co-member. ?What If! is focused on retaining this open culture. Recruitment is based in the first instance on attitude not aptitude, and selection is most concerned with recruiting staff from a variety of backgrounds as friends, not colleagues. Underlying this is a desire to create a workforce consisting of a broad church of people with wildly differing backgrounds and life experiences, but the same passion for creating ideas and putting them into practice. This makes good business sense as it means that they are able to offer consulting services from individuals with whom the client companies would not normally have contact.

The aim of ?What If! is to breathe a spirit of creativity and entre-preneurism into companies. It acts as a consultant to a myriad of different organizations, primarily in the retail and fast-moving consumer goods industries, but increasingly in governmental and not-for-profit sectors. It is committed to developing tangible results from a creative input, believing firmly that if an idea does not result in anything tangible such as a new product, marketing campaign or cultural change, it is of little value.

The company has also created a £1 million fund designed to attract business ideas from would-be entrepreneurs both inside and outside the company. The message is simple: ?What If! is open to considering any business ideas, no matter how outlandish they may appear. The company is successfully exploiting the fact that by operating out of a big-business structure, new businesses can be launched at significantly lower cost than most organizations will spend researching an idea, and in half the time.

One of the most frequently asked tasks of ?What *If!* is how to bring client companies closer to consumers as individuals. The methods vary. On one occasion, the company 'hired' a high street for the day to take a client team on a realistic shopping experience. They have also invited consumers to get involved in the planning stages of new product launches, in areas such as budgeting. The company also runs a division called 'Consumer TV', which puts together films to distil the facts, ideas and concepts behind the reports and information that client companies already have at their fingertips. This provides a greater level of consumer insight and puts new ways of presenting and interpreting consumer information at the forefront of a company's thinking.

Venture peoplism

Venture peoplism denotes the provision of capital and human resources to co-members within (or without) the organization who have the ability to develop ideas and the ability to set them up and run them, with the company retaining a share of the venture.

There has traditionally existed a dichotomy between the entrepreneurial spirit and the corporate machine. The aim of venture peoplism is for organizations to act as incubators for entrepreneurs, by internalizing them and encouraging their talents. Rather than going it alone, these 'intrapreneurs' are supported by the organization and have access to its people, experience, knowledge, finance structure, systems and processes in the pursuit of their ideas. Crucially, they are reassured of their job security, even if their proposed idea or project is unsuccessful. The resources for venture peoplist projects can come from several sources, including revenue investment, which would be tax efficient while increasing the value of the venture peoplist business as a whole.

Retaining an entrepreneur as an intrapreneur

Venture peoplism throws up a number of issues to be dealt with by the HR director, including how to retain someone who by their very nature may not want to have a 'boss'. It is also important to encourage staff to express their latent abilities within your company in the first place. How do you decide who to support and how to support them?

Corporate incubators have been heralded as a new competitive weapon. While the cynic would identify such a scheme as a way of exploiting the intellectual resources of a team purely for corporate gain, the innovative talent manager recognizes it as a means of nurturing and retaining creative talent, even after the dotcom bubble has burst. HR must have systems to encourage intrapreneurs, coach them and empower them to manage their own ventures, so that they stay and add value to the company, and help it to grow organically. Without such support, the would-be entrepreneurs will slip out of the door, taking their creativity and ideas with them.

An early example of this from Reed is our foray into online temporary recruitment, in the form of TempJobs. Four of our co-members saw an opportunity to get the organization into the online temp market more quickly than our competitors could do it. We were happy to support the venture, in view of the benefit that it could potentially bring to the company. TempJobs did not, in fact, work out as planned, and never really got off the ground. However, the factor that marks this venture out as a success for peoplism is the fact that all of those involved in TempJobs were welcomed back into Reed; not as failures, to be shunted into meaningless positions, but as successes who were still capable of attaining great things within Reed. They have all gone on to make the most of their learning experience, and have been able to reach director level in the organization within a few years.

The benefit for the parent organization is clear. Despite the fact that this venture failed, Reed gained from the learning experience of the individuals, and retained co-members who have gone on to be stars for the company. If they had not been allowed to do this as intrapreneurs, Reed may well have lost their talent for good, something that no organization can afford to do.

According to Andy Gaule, who runs the Henley-Incubator at Henley Management College, about 50 venture peoplist start-ups are either in place or being developed by large companies. Most of these are UK based.[62] Although only a small percentage of the ideas submitted is likely to make it through rigorous financial scrutiny to action stage, non-actioned ideas are still incredibly valuable to the company. In an era where innovation defines success, all concepts, creations and inceptions add value to the parent company, whether implemented or not. Equally important to the company are the individuals whose ventures do not succeed.

So how can you implement this policy in your own organization, if no facility for generating new business ideas is already in place? One possibility is the route taken by Reed. In 2002 the second of our 'Who Wants to be a Millionaire' competitions was launched, inviting co-members to submit a proposal for a new business unit that they believe they could run and bring into profit within 24 months. The initial submission is a summary of the idea, supported by a profit and loss statement to show that the financial projections are feasible, and a personal statement, outlining how the co-member, as an individual, has the attributes necessary to make his or her idea a success. The process then continues with the submission of a more detailed business plan from the longlist selected, and the presentation of shortlisted ideas to the chief executive. The winner of the first competition was Reed Property Appointments, which is now up and running in Bristol, placing property and estate management professionals into employment. Although progress here has been slower than we had hoped, owing to recent trading conditions, the business is gradually getting off the ground, and we are committed to giving the two co-members involved a fair amount of time to make it a success. The commitment to seeing these ventures through, with a guarantee that the idea will not be dropped in panic if it is not an instant success, is an essential part of venture peoplist policy.

We decided to run the Millionaire competition for a second time because we could see the benefits it brought to both individuals and the company. Individual co-members are encouraged to think outside their normal sphere, and have the potential, effectively, to start their own company, with all the learning opportunities, challenges and personal development that that entails, but without the fear of being left with nothing if things do not go to plan. Reed has, of course, a potentially successful new business unit and an extension of its market share. We can also offer our most talented staff the chance to use their talents fully, and show that our words – our public commitment to an enterprising culture – are backed up by our actions.

A case in point: Reed Health Group

Reed Health Group is a great example of successful venture peoplism. The group started as Reed Nurse, part of the Reed Executive group, in the mid-1960s. It has since expanded, launching Reed Paramedic (later to become Reed Health Professionals) in 1984 and Reed Social Care in 1988. These are all prime examples of talent within the organization seeing opportunities in the market and being given the space and funding to develop into successful business concerns.

Reed Health Group demerged from Reed Executive in 2001. This would seem, at first glance, to make it a failed example of venture peoplism, from our point of view at least. Surely a demerged venture represents the loss of the stars that we aim to retain? This is not the case; the key to successful venture peoplism is knowing when to let go. RHG made a good name for itself within the health-care market, benefiting Reed Executive through the extension of our brand. However, Reed Executive has grown organically from the original single branch to the current 283 branches, and this is a policy we intend to continue. The nature of the healthcare market, in contrast, is such that the management of Reed Health Group feels that it needs to grow by acquisition if the group is to succeed in gaining a large market share. This point of divergence is where common sense dictates that the intrapreneurial venture is ready to go it alone. A demerger such as ours, with no acrimony, and an agreed business relationship for the future, is the ultimate peoplist success. The parent company gave the venture space to grow, and did not let possessiveness over the origins of RHG cloud the development of the best strategy for the company.

There can be no prescriptive approach to introducing venture peoplism to your organization. It works because it is not prescriptive, because it relies on the innovative approach of individuals. Give your talented individuals the chance to come up with some ideas. If they can demonstrate feasibility, allow them to put those ideas into practice. Stand back and watch the ideas develop: watch motivation improve, keep your stars committed and happy, and let your business and badge grow.

The thinking is ...

Bland and generalistic human resource management strategies are as purposeful and successful as trying to herd cats. The challenge is to individualize strategies in order to channel co-members' talents to achieve corporate objectives for as long as is mutually desired. Companies must actively encourage, and use, as much creativity, innovation and enthusiasm as possible, and have procedures in place to drive forward and reward those who add the most value. Two key strategies for future success are to recruit individuals who are intuitively intelligent, and to strive continually to boost the corporate libido.

CHAPTER 6

Numerical dyslexia

Accountancy was in crisis long before the scandal of the demise of Andersen Consulting, the Enron bankruptcy and the deception at WorldCom rocked corporate America. However, the profession's position as a valuable indication of company success is even more precarious now.

People confer lasting competitive advantage. Accounting measures provide scant information about the key assets of the peoplist economy and, consequently, the companies in which they reside. Accounting systems are slow and historic; our economy is progressive and unpredictable. The real sources of competitive advantage – creativity, enterprise and innovation – are currently undetectable in audited accounts.

A fresh look at accounting is required. This chapter outlines how companies can drive success by measuring intangibles. It illustrates how to develop profit : enterprise ratios and create a management dashboard.

Accounting procedures must evolve significantly to regain the relevancy lost in the transition to the peoplist economy. In truth, accountancy did not even serve capitalism well. Accounting tools have not fully fitted the needs of the day since the Middle Ages, when the rhythm of the annual cycles and harvests of the agricultural economy suited the production of annual double-entry accounts. Major problems arise in understanding not only the value of companies, but also the processes by which that value is calculated. The inadequacy of the system is clear from the tremendous vulnerability in market-to-book ratios, i.e. the gap between the share price of a company and its tangible asset base on the balance sheet. Between 1990 and 1995 the average market-to-book ratio of American listed companies increased from 149 to 202 per cent. This pattern is particularly obvious in the new industries. In 1993, while 30 American cellular telephone companies had negative cash-flows, their total market value was $34 billion, giving a median market-to-book ratio of 12, six times the corresponding ratio for industrial companies.[63] E-commerce valuations have turned tradition upside down. Companies with no track record, virtually no tangible assets and zero profits (even those with no prospect of profits in the foreseeable future, as has been the case with Freeserve) have been valued to the tune of hundreds of millions of pounds. The online bookshop Amazon, which broke into the black for the first time in 2002, was valued on the Nasdaq at an astonishing $50 billion long before it broke into profit.[64]

Historical performance (let us not forget that in the future economy a growing number of companies will have a very limited history indeed) often has little bearing on how a company will perform in the future. This is particularly relevant in the current business environment of perpetual instability, as evidenced by the demise of brands in Chapter 3.

Serious consequences

Businesses are not speaking the truth, not hearing the truth and not seeing the truth about their value drivers. The components of the accounting system are inadequate and out of date. There is a rhetoric–reality gap in modern business. Much is said about the importance of key workers, the value of brands and the influence of marketing. Yet, when it comes to measuring and presenting the performance of these key drivers, the vast majority of companies neglect intangibles. There are three reasons for this: bad management, confusion over how to garner the information, and the prohibitive structure of accounts and reports. There is no meaningful measure of the intangible items such as co-member commitment and trust, which make up more than 70 per cent of the value of FTSE 350 companies.[65] The consequences for firms are considerable. Until investors have all of the information they need, both financial and non-financial, they will be unable to achieve optimal allocation of resources across firms. If they do not have that information, they will under-value their stock. Where attempts to measure intangibles are made, the method by which they are valued remains a mystery, with ad hoc and arbitrary figures plucked out by accountants struggling to stay relevant in the people economy.

According to a recent PricewaterhouseCoopers survey, less than 20 per cent of investors and analysts regard financial reports as very useful. Less than 40 per cent of companies find their own financial reports to be very useful! Around 20 per cent of investors and analysts, and 10 per cent of companies, perceive financial reports to be either not very, or not at all, useful. Let us not underestimate the scale of this problem; four out of five British companies fail to report on the assets that provide their main source of competitive advantage. Companies are measuring the wrong inputs and wrong outputs. Companies are in crisis as a direct result of poor accounting.

An Ernst & Young survey of 275 portfolio managers from all major types of institutional investors and funds showed that one-third of the information used to justify investment decisions is non-financial.[66] Such is the enervation of accounting practice that a frustrated 64 per cent of American managers have reported that their companies are actively experimenting with new ways of measuring, collecting and reporting non-financial data.

Budgets are of dubious value

It is incredibly difficult to visualize your business a year in advance with any precision. Progressive companies have consequently dropped detailed budgets in favour of scenario planning. Scenario planning, which involves devising tactics and visualizing outcomes for any number of political, legal, economic and business eventualities should be refreshed as relevant.

Balance sheets are redundant

Balance sheets, for centuries the bedrock of accounting, are too backward looking. The only useful value displayed on a balance sheet is cash or near-cash resources and liabilities. Because creativity kills capital, items such as factories or equipment can be killed off very quickly by becoming obsolete since innovation and technology are continually producing better ways of doing things. In 1999 an incredible 76 per cent of the 226 quoted companies analysed did not record any intangibles on their balance sheet.[67] Success is all about balancing resilience; resilience should be in the balance sheet, and the results in the profit and loss accounts.

Profit and loss is fallible

It is common business practice to use current profits for revenue investment. In the past, companies would have built factories or offices and capitalized these assets, leaving the profit and loss account unaffected. Now, investment for the majority of businesses inevitably means revenue investment, which does affect profit, and is also tax-effective. Expenditure on advertising, training, and research and development will result in a drop in profit as those costs are accounted for. In 1997, the internet services provider America OnLine was fined and criticized by the regulatory authorities after it accounted for its marketing spend as an asset rather than a cost. But can the accountancy profession really justify classifying advertising as a cost as opposed to an investment? The value of research and development invested in a software program or the value of a user base of an internet shopping site should be quantifiable. At present it is not, and therefore a wealth of financial and strategic decisions is being made without access to relevant and reliable information.

The traditional bottom line is worthless

The bottom line can easily be affected by exceptional gains

and losses, additions in the footnotes and countless other tricks for massaging the figures. Hidden factors such as delayed or brought-forward invoicing can heavily influence the reported figures. While profit margin is used as an indicator of how attractive it may be to invest money in a company, it does not reveal much about the loyalty of customers or the efficiency of employees. It may not even value work in progress. Indeed, the margin itself may be misleading.

Driving success by valuing intangibles

Businesses cannot measure everything, but it is imperative that companies have the tools to isolate and measure those intangible assets that drive their value. Choosing the right criteria is absolutely fundamental to avoid data-rich/information-poor scenarios. Measuring performance is only of use when the results are translated into action.

Although there is no common approach, performance measurement models are being developed by companies to try to track the role of intangibles in generating financial results. The question is how these measures, and the different approaches taken by progressive companies, should be developed and integrated so as to provide the most reliable information framework for your organization.

Integrate non-financial information with the strategic story of your organization and relevant financial data. Any new system must complement the body of your management information system. Provide forward-looking information that is targeted towards a specific outcome, for example increasing shareholder value, informing employees and building links with the community.

Deliver a clear and consistent message across media and stakeholder groups. Avoid selective disclosure, and provide the same message to investors and analysts in your financial report as you would through other available media, including interim communications, investor and analyst briefings, and the internet.

Karl Erik Sveiby's 'Intangible Assets Monitor'

One model that has been developed and used by a number of progressive companies, particularly in Sweden, is Sveiby's 'Intangible Assets Monitor'. The virtue of the monitor, which is used alongside conventional financial reports, lies in its flexibility, meaning that companies in different industries can adopt it. The model divides intangible assets into three main categories:

- External structures, consisting of relationships with customers and suppliers, brand names, trademarks and reputation. The value of these assets is primarily influenced by how well the company handles its relationships with outside stakeholders such as customers and suppliers.

- Internal structures, covering patents, concepts, models and computer and administrative systems. Also included among the internal structures are the informal organization, internal networks, and the organization's 'culture' or 'spirit'.

■ Co-member competence, referring to people's capacity to act in various work-based situations. Measurements include skill, education, experience, values and social skills.

Sveiby then analyses these intangible assets according to four criteria:

■ operational efficiency

■ growth

■ renewal

■ stability.

The aim is to gain a perspective on how the intangible assets are developing, by designing indicators that correlate with the growth of the asset in question, its renewal rate and how efficiently a company is utilizing it.

A model based along these lines could be incorporated into a new company balance sheet, which would encompass the traditional financial information and also focus on reporting and measuring intangible assets. Accounts should be consolidated and averaged over a 3-year period, to indicate the recent trends in the business, and to make clear the direction in which your company is moving.

Co-member measurements

The fact that people, and not capital, are the main revenue creators is ignored by accountancy. Success is no longer about ownership; companies cannot 'own' individuals as they did capital.

Measuring the impact of human resource (HR) policies is an achievable goal for all employers, and one that is necessary to maximize the use of key resources. Straightforward measurements may include the levels of education, IQ and competence of employees, expenditures on training, employee turnover and length of tenure with the company. A commitment to measuring and reporting the attitudes and competences of employees is further encouraged by research which states that 78 per cent of investors regard 'employee productivity' measures as being particularly valuable in making investment decisions.[68]

Employee effectiveness should also be measured. One option is to divide employees into different competence levels according to the value they add to your organization, such as the first class, business class and economy class. Measure their input as such.

The cost of recruitment and turnover is a simple HR measurement. Determine the optimum percentage level of staff turnover and periodically benchmark against it. As with all information, you need to know your constant or your benchmark; if the turnover is too low the company may lack dynamism, if it is too high it is also indicative of a problem. Strive to be as detailed as possible; turnover in terms of internal promotion and retirement may, or may not be less damaging than turnover to competitors. Measurements are only of use when the results are used to enhance performance, therefore companies should set strategic targets for each measurement and compare the results with the performance of those who made the initial decision to recruit.

As a company, boast about how much salaries have increased, as much as you boast about the increase in share value.

Since the early 1990s, we have seen a huge growth in the appreciation of and demand for knowledge management strategies, with senior management eager to draw on the latent knowledge embedded within company employees. Of greater importance are enterprise management strategies, as knowledge is merely a product of learning and confers little competitive advantage in the internet age. An enterprise management strategy at its most basic should encompass a formal process to solicit and gather enterprising ideas, a database or intranet direction to showcase concepts, an integrated reward system, the facility for objective feedback and a supportive culture that provides resources for enterprising behaviours.

Organizations should strive to measure the value added by each employee. The method of calculation is very much context dependent, but may be derived from sales figures, contracts won, appraisals from line managers, feedback from internal and external customers, ideas for organizational improvements submitted and so on. The aim is not to spend too much time on achieving an over-detailed figure to represent each employee, but to have a sound idea of how each individual is doing across a number of key indicators. This is particularly relevant in times of downturn when, as we have seen, short-sighted management often cuts talent.

By reporting on the tools used to manage people, including the provision for performance reviews, profit:enterprise ratios, and training and development plans, your organization demonstrates that is serious about listening to and developing co-members, characteristics that young professionals look for. Companies must communicate co-member strategy, explaining how co-members are managed in accordance with the core values and fundamentals.

Paying attention to the results of employee surveys clearly helps management to gain an understanding of the views of the workforce. There are other commercial benefits too. This kind of information not only helps external stakeholder groups to gauge the opinions of the workforce, but also helps outsiders to judge the performance of management in communicating their message to the workforce.

Customer-focused measurements

Investment in customers in the form of loyalty cards and bonuses can yield significant gains in the future. Developments in technology enable accurate measurement of the effectiveness of acquisition costs and customer retention spending. Moreover, a reliable estimate of the value of each customer is possible, by calculating the expected revenue from an average customer. Many of the fastest growing sectors in the new economy – internet, cable and cellular industries – are investing heavily in customer acquisition. As we have seen, these costs are treated as an immediate expense rather than an investment in the future, fuelling the irrelevancy of financial accounts. Over 70 per cent of investors regard 'customer retention' information as particularly valuable in making investment decisions.[69] However, beware of miscalculating prospects as customers, at best they are moving shots.

Importantly, companies should also measure the profitability of their customers: if 20 per cent of customers contribute 80 per cent of revenue, organizations must be aware of this so that they can adopt a retention strategy to suit.

Companies must have the confidence to lose and avoid promiscuous or costly customers and concentrate on keeping the kind of customers they want: those that produce profit.

Levels of customer satisfaction measurements cover factors such as the average speed of complaint resolution and the average number of complaints per customer (of vital importance in service-orientated businesses). In addition, by measuring the number of repeat customers and customer feedback on price and quality, organizations are able to garner a good indication of future acceptance.

Cost of customer acquisition, cost per customer, average spend per customer, average tenure per customer and cost of customer maintenance are also key performance indicators.

A case in point: Coloplast

The Copenhagen-based medical supplies company Coloplast produces an 'Intellectual Capital Account' which encompasses detailed information on maximizing customer satisfaction. They measure their performance and calculate their future strategy on the basis of what they call their 'missions'. These are: empathy with user needs, innovation, reliability of supplier, quality of life and maximum customer satisfaction. The company sets out to show how each one of these missions will be achieved. For example, under 'innovation' the company stresses in its 2000 Annual Report:

20 per cent of products must be new products. It is our objective to generate 20 per cent of turnover from new products – defined as products less than four years old – because such an objective guarantees a high focus on innovation. With several successful product launches this year, the ratio of new products is expected to be more than 20 per cent next year.

After establishing the methods used to enable each of the 'missions' to be achieved, tables give figures on the success, or otherwise, in meeting these tasks. The figures given cover a 3-year period so that the onlooker can establish a far greater indication of the relative health of the company, beyond the traditional report which covers progress only over the preceding financial year. Future objectives are set for each separate mission, with specific targets, detailed for levels of innovation, customer satisfaction and so on, being set for the next year.

Environmental reporting

As individual power grows, companies will have to realign their corporate values away from profit alone. Environmental issues, social responsibility and ethical considerations of concern to the stakeholder will play a greater role. The challenge facing companies is to go beyond strictly financial measures and to identify and report on the dynamics of value within that company. Environmental reporting is influenced by the recognition that a company's ability to recruit and retain staff and customers, and therefore create future value, depends largely on Camelot public standing and reputation.

Many companies focus on social auditing based on their responsibilities to their stakeholders. One such company is Camelot, which gives a wealth of information on what it is doing to maintain and improve its relationships with its various stakeholders. A large amount of data is given on Camelot's dialogue with 'community stakeholders', including a breakdown of how funds are distributed within the community. The report then assesses the performance of Camelot against the Quality Scoring Framework (QSF). This is based on eight quality principles of social and ethical accounting, auditing and reporting: communication, external verification, continuous improvement, completeness, comparability, inclusivity, evolutionary and embeddedness. These have been developed by New Economics and adapted by the Institute of Social and Ethical Account Ability to form AA1000, its voluntary accountability standard. The QSF breaks down the eight principles into a further 56 criteria, seven for each principle. In assessing the quality of an organization's social accounting process, each criterion is rated on a scale of 0 (not satisfied at all) to 4 (satisfied to a high extent). The scores are then totalled for each principle and mapped against New Economic Five-Stage Model.

Essentially, if an investor or analyst wanted to calculate the true value of Camelot, this would not be possible without an appreciation of the relationships that Camelot has with its many stakeholders; the true importance of the QSF is that it fills that information vacuum, but in the final event it could all disappear if Camelot fails to renew its contract in 2006.[69]

The importance of environmental and social audits is context dependent, but all organizations should make some mention of them in their accounts in order to give stakeholders a rounded view of the organization. Companies should also aim to measure internal innovation by tracking the number of new processes implemented in areas such as administration and accounts.

A case in point: The Furniture Resource Centre Group (FRCG)

Founded in 1988, the FRCG is a small but rapidly growing social business operating in the Merseyside area, which reduced its income from social grants from 29 per cent of income in 1996 to only 1.5 per cent in 2002.

At FRCG, the focus is on marrying the ethos of social enterprise, traditionally run at the junction between charitable and government sectors, with the profit imperative of the commercial world. The company is led by CEO Liam Black. The group makes money; over the accounting year 2000–01, they succeeded in increasing turnover by 16 per cent to over £6 million, and profitability by 26 per cent.

FRCG consists of three separate businesses. At the heart of the group is the 'Furniture Resource Centre', which provides a one-stop-shop furnishing service to registered landlords throughout England and Wales. 'Revive', opened in 1998, retails furniture direct to the public. In 2000, the group launched 'Bulky Bob's', a furniture recycling company. FRCG was the first company in the UK to be nominated for New Economics Foundation Inner City 100 Index, and was rated by the Index as the fastest growing social enterprise in Britain in 2001.

Social auditing

FRCG has put a huge amount of internal energy into developing social accounting which shows the value of the company's relationships with its various stakeholders, and aims to uncover the real impact of the business on the lives of customers and co-members. This is viewed as essential to an organization that measures its value not simply in terms of pounds and pence, but also by the contribution it makes to the low-income families that purchase its merchandise.

FRCG audits its social activity in part by asking difficult questions that sometimes highlight failings or weaknesses. The social accounts are published in a document entitled 'Proving It', which outlines far more than the company's commercial growth, and attempts to audit the social activity and organizational values that underpin all commercial activity.

Below are some of the social, community and relationship-building activities contained within the Proving It booklet:

■ An award for the company's supplier of the year. Further research indicates that 100 per cent of suppliers believe that FRCG sets clear and agreed objectives, while 86 per cent said they were easy to do business with.

- Research conducted by an independent body which reveals general characteristics of the FRCG customer base, indicating for example that 36 per cent had been in conditions of homelessness during their lives.

- Information relating to how customers were attracted to the company and details on who they are. For instance, a survey of the customer base highlighted that 60 per cent were female, half were aged between 20 and 40, and 16 per cent were disabled.

- Employee feedback on how well the company lives up to its stated values of creativity, bravery, professionalism and passion, as well as statistics showing what the workforce gets out of working with the group both emotionally and developmentally.

Profit: enterprise ratios

For many years company valuations have been judged and compared on the basis of price to earnings ratios (P/Es). These are inadequate in an economic climate of perpetual instability, where past successes are no guarantee of future performance. A better indicator of future performance is to develop profit: enterprise ratios, which show the proportion of profits derived from new ideas and processes. These will be the P/Es of the future.

A first shot at arriving at a P/E might be to allocate the profit you have made over a set period to different generations of product innovations and ideas. For example, the ratio might be worked out as follows.

Each £1 000 000 continuing profit (excluding one-off gains) might be divisible as:

- £500 000 from products or services in place for over 10 years

- £300 000 from products or services in place for 5–10 years, e.g. internet-generated sales from a company website

- £100 000 from products introduced between 3 and 5 years ago, e.g. a new line or complementary service

- £100 000 from recent innovations that have been in place for less than 3 years.

Within the Reed Group our total profit is generated by the branch network, some of which has been in place for over 40 years, by our website and by the success of relatively new recruitment specialisms such as Reed Education or Reed Marketing. The idea is to favour profit derived from recent innovations while discounting profits from cash cows. Therefore, profits from business processes that have been in existence for over 10 years are divided by 2, while profits from newer innovations are multiplied in acknowledgement of their potential, as well as current, value. Profits derived from processes in place between 5 and 10 years remain neutral. Thus, the calculation continues like this:

10 years+:	£500 000 is divided by 2, giving £250 000
5–10 years:	£300 000 remains neutral
3–5 years:	£100 000 is multiplied by 5, giving £500 000
0–3 years:	£100 000 is multiplied by 6, giving £600 000

These figures are totalled, giving £1 650 000, and set in ratio to the total profit of £1 000 000, giving us a final P/E of 1.65.

Given a bit of thought, companies can improve on this basic model to develop and tailor a profit:enterprise ratio that meets their needs.

Creating your own management dashboard

A management dashboard records and displays the indicators that are key to the success of your business in a format that permits easy consideration. The business environment is in a state of flux, and it is difficult to keep an eye on everything at all times. Thus, the key indicators should be tailored to your organization for frequent analysis by your senior management triumvirate. Any changes or deviations can quickly and easily be noted, and will be actioned swiftly if they are of sufficient concern to warrant a warning light. The information should be of an appropriate level that management can scan to gain an overview of the state of play, as a car driver does in checking that all is well.

Ethiopiaid is a charity that raises money for projects in Addis Ababa. From its management dashboard (Figure 2) it is possible for the manager of the charity to keep tabs on the key indicators that are vital to achieving its goals.

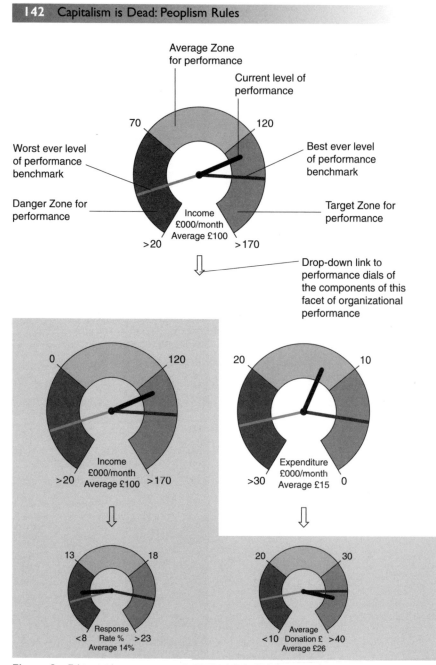

Figure 2   Ethiopiaid management dashboard (*continued opposite*).

The Ethiopiaid dashboard has the following key features.

Four principal indicators:

■ income

■ expenditure

■ donor base

■ donor care.

It is advisable to have at least one non-financial principal indicator, in order to form the fullest picture possible. In the case of Ethiopiaid, the dials indicating the increase, or

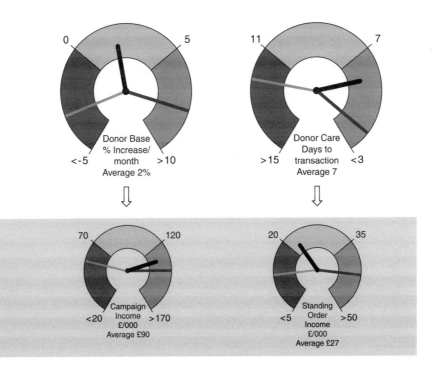

otherwise, in donor (customer) base and donor care are crucially important to the success of the charity.

Each principal indicator drops down into four supporting indicators. For income, these are:

■ response rate to mailings

■ average donation per campaign

■ campaign income in total

■ income from standing orders.

On each dial, set benchmark parameters of the best ever reading and the worst prior reading, so you can see how current performance compares with previous results. The acceptable ranges should be displayed in a different colour.

Corporate black boxes would appear to be another option on the road of increasing managerial accountability post-Enron. These could be used to record senior-level decision making, enabling inquiries after collapses to pinpoint accountability.

The thinking is ...

Closing balance

Some viable alternatives to the redundant accounting system that fails to measure key value drivers have been set out in this chapter. Aspects of traditional financial information still have a part to play, but they must be complemented by information and measurements of those intangibles that determine business success. Only by doing so can business performance be accurately measured and appropriate company valuations made. The speed of change has caught many unawares, and organizations cannot afford to have any key value drivers hidden in blind spots; it is therefore wise to construct a comprehensive management dashboard from which to steer progress.

CHAPTER 7

ICT: innovative use of communications and technology

Companies must be both proactive and responsive in order to ensure that individual preferences are met. New information and communications technology has changed the focus of marketing. Technology provides the capacity through which companies can target individual customers to an ever-greater degree. As a result, companies tread a fine line between technological innovation, excessive marketing and stakeholder dislocation. This chapter demonstrates how internal and external communications can be reassessed and refocused to fulfil corporate goals, and illustrates how innovative use of technology led corporate strategy within our company's recruitment website, reed.co.uk.

Back markets, not marketing

Before we progress to look at innovative communications and technology, it is necessary to outline the two main reasons why marketing is no longer an efficient or effective business tool. The first point was established in Chapter 3: as the provision of goods evolves from narrow brands to badges, communication to consumers evolves from marketing to public relations (PR). The second reason involves the acceptance that marketing is simply too slow in an environment that changes so rapidly. Thus, companies should abandon marketing, and concentrate instead on PR and markets.

Clued-up companies will watch out for swiftly changing societal and demographic trends with a keen interest, as some traditional markets shrink and opportunities develop in previously unconsidered areas. For example, marketers have identified 'Kiddles' as a key target for the next decade. A facet of the naked individual, kiddles are the new demographic of 35–45-year-old childless professionals who have significant levels of disposable income to spend on leisure activities. Conversely, the under-30s, traditionally a consumer group with high levels of disposable income, are the first generation to be poorer than their parents are. 'Tweenagers' have also emerged as a key group, encompassing those between childhood and teenage years. This group is more affluent than ever as a result of the decrease in the number of children per family, and the increase in dual-income households. They are highly media literate and a greater emphasis is being placed on them as a result of their influence on parental purchasing power.

Many companies are trying to increase their market share by covering two ends of a market at once, as J Sainsbury's is doing by relaunching its Savacentre brand to target younger, less affluent families in addition to the demographic targeted by its original stores. Yet there are problems in diversifying, as main competitors Tesco and Asda already have a strong value-for-money badge reputation covering two markets under one roof.

The real goal for companies is to break into new markets. These are where the real opportunities for strategic expansion lie since, in our information-saturated age, the ubiquity of advertising means that marketing has lost its edge for all but the most innovative campaigns.

Communication management strategies

One of the most pressing challenges facing companies is how to develop and maintain a communication management strategy (CMS) in a marketplace glutted with information. Consumers are flooded with news, offers and data through a wealth of communication channels. Managing information through selection and filtration is essential for both internal and external marketing. Internally, networks need to be developed, as sharing information and connections with others can reduce the burden on the individual, preventing the oversaturation that leads to attention deficit. Externally, the system must make provision for the small criticisms that can cause crisis when widely disseminated. Already, chain e-mails have caused health scares and PR damage to a significant number of companies and products, ranging from claims that certain antiperspirants can lead to cancer, to alleged links between some brands of cooking oil and mustard gas. Nearly 75 per cent of 600 prominent US chief executives surveyed admitted they were concerned by the

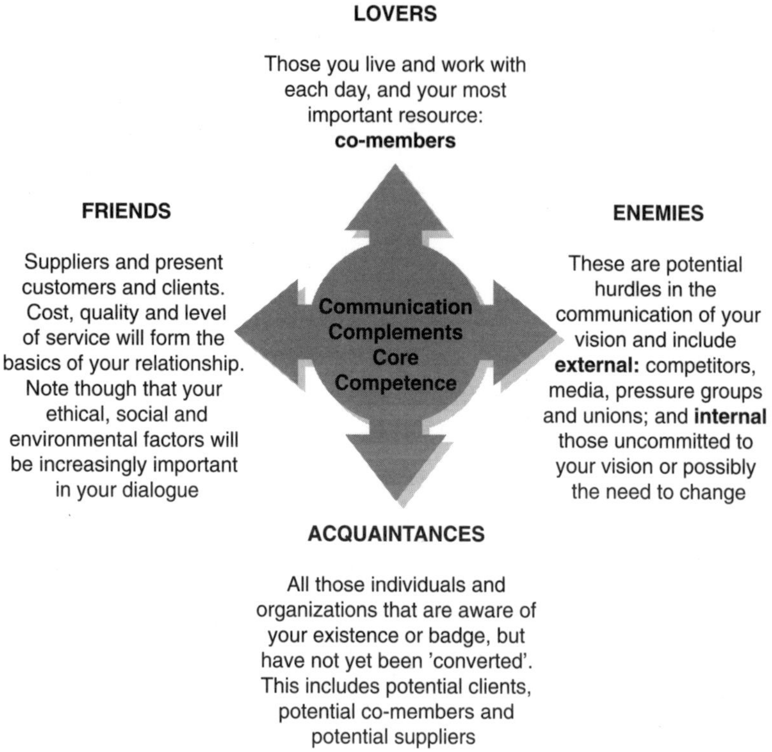

LOVERS

Those you live and work with
each day, and your most
important resource:
co-members

FRIENDS

Suppliers and present
customers and clients.
Cost, quality and level
of service will form the
basics of your relationship.
Note though that your
ethical, social and
environmental factors will
be increasingly important
in your dialogue

**Communication
Complements
Core
Competence**

ENEMIES

These are potential
hurdles in the
communication of your
vision and include
external: competitors,
media, pressure groups
and unions; and **internal**
those uncommitted to
your vision or possibly
the need to change

ACQUAINTANCES

All those individuals and
organizations that are aware of
your existence or badge, but
have not yet been 'converted'.
This includes potential clients,
potential co-members and
potential suppliers

Figure 3   Leaf model.

mounting dissemination of negative information over the internet, yet only 50 per cent have strategies in place for managing internet communications.[70]

Any form of information management must be placed in context of business objectives. More information is not better information; mass amounts of data simply act to clog up the managerial brain and cloud decision making. Business trends are often non-linear, chaotic and volatile, with market needs changing at a seemingly ever-increasing pace, meaning that predicting the future is difficult. In order to survive, let alone prosper, therefore, company management is required to marry the information at its disposal with something much cruder but nonetheless crucial: gut instinct. The people with the keenest gut instincts will be those closest to the action, not necessarily senior management (see intuitive intelligence in Chapter 5).

The attention market, that is the ability of companies to relay their message to a receptive audience, is so competitive that the real challenge is for organizations to get their messages heard. A trend is emerging of consumers being paid to give their attention in bids to induce them to sign up for long-term contracts. This can be seen with mobile phone companies, a market that is in danger of becoming saturated. Companies gladly give away the manufactured hardware which is of little relative value, such as the handsets and the power-chargers, to get a consumer to sign up to a contract. The consumer is then bound by that contract to the service provider for the medium term, which also gives the companies access to communicate and market new innovations to them.

Communication failure can destroy a business. In an era when information and data can be transferred in an instant, the inability to communicate effectively spells disaster. Speed and accuracy are of the essence.

Internal communications are becoming increasingly important as the views of co-members become ever more central to the success of the company. Electronic messages and company intranets are necessary, as part of the vital lifeblood carriers in the new peoplist economy. In a survey of major British companies, 67 per cent had internal and external communicators working together in the same corporate communications department. The report, by Watson Helsby, indicates that an increasing number of CEOs are beginning to understand the commercial value of employee communications.[71]

Some companies are recruiting a new breed of managers to defend their reputations proactively. These communications managers are constantly on-call. News is round-the-clock and real-time, so companies must ensure that they have eloquent and informed communications managers to deal with problems as they arise.

Technology-based targeting

New networks and technology are rendering traditional communication channels redundant. The *Blair Witch Project*, a low-budget American movie, became a world phenomenon in 2000 through a co-ordinated email and web-based marketing strategy, at a fraction of the cost of traditional marketing methods. Not so long ago, companies had to communicate the same message to everyone, with very limited opportunity for those customers to provide feedback. Be receptive and adventurous to the new avenues of marketing and communication that are opened up by technology. The power of the computer chip doubles every year and bandwidth is continually expanding, enabling more content to be received by more people. In 1993 there were only 50 sites on the worldwide web. In 2002 there are well over 350 million, rising to an estimated 709 million by 2004, according to projections by *eMarketer*. The main increases will come from developing countries, for example the number of new users in Latin

America will grow by almost 40 per cent annually between 2000 and 2004, while the number of new users in North America will grow at a slower rate of 14.3 per cent.

The internet remains a threat to the core business of many service industries owing to the inevitable disintermediation between the consumer and the product or service. In the recruitment industry, this means that because the internet allows job seekers to connect and apply directly to the employer, it removes the need for traditional intermediary channels and their associated costs and delays. The internet has changed the role of the intermediaries. In the past, companies needed them to attract candidates, but now the internet provides so many applicants that intermediaries have been repositioned into sifting applicants. Amazon.com is a prime example of an internet company thriving from disintermediation, and its success in the book business has caused much consternation in many other industries. One of the most high-profile examples of a company benefiting from disintermediation was Napster, which cut the music store, the recording industry and the artist out of the loop, and gave the consumer the most direct access to music possible.

The online market has the capacity to dent the profits of many. A survey of 1700 firms found that two-thirds of businesses promote themselves on the web, but only 3 per cent claim to have registered a significant increase in turnover as a result. Just 10 per cent of firms take payments over the internet and 63 per cent cannot receive web orders.[72] The simple lesson about the utility of the internet must be learnt: use it to augment and improve rather than eclipse your traditional business model.

Novel schemes such as 'PayPal', which enable customers to email payments to companies or to each other quickly, easily and securely, are becoming popular stateside. As most of the e-commerce done on the web is currently financed by credit cards, a development that is likely to impact on business in the near future is the application of the principle of pre-payment to finance web transactions. Some, or all, of the following new technologies may be used by companies to improve their communication processes.

■ The automation of customer services in the next 3–5 years will make the provision of consumer-friendly services more challenging.

■ Context-aware services (that is, systems which provide information according to where you are and what you are doing) will allow more information to be collated for customer profiles.

■ Embedded sensors, which are computers built into everyday items, will offer more channels for communication and customer feedback.

■ Voice response, where a consumer is able to talk to a computer over the phone, and it responds, will have a major impact on the service sector. This system works without keyboards and internet connections, via a telephone. It could be the future of customer feedback and has already been experimented with by Virgin Trains to speed up the booking process.

These new channels allow greater and quicker measurement of response and tracking of customer spending and retention, enabling communication to become a fully measured and costed business process, rather than the hit-or-miss marketing costings of the past. Marketing via new technological channels can be complicated and the rapidity of innovation, together with the pressure to be among the first to exploit developments, brings enormous challenges at both strategic and administrative levels. Thinking and acting in double-quick time is a vital component of successful communication.

A common example of where this hurdle has proved impassable thus far is with customer relationship management (CRM) systems. These systems are designed to deliver a holistic view over all the customers in an organization, providing projections on future activity and analysis on spending data. CRM systems cover all interaction with consumers, from initial approaches through advertising, to response rates, purchasing and invoicing. The expense is significant, with programmes costing up to £70 million each and taking an average of 2 years to implement. Over half (55 per cent) of technological CRM programmes fail. As many as one in five CRM users have admitted that their initiative had actually made customer relations worse.[73] The simple message is that companies have to get behind the measurement and offer best value to the consumer.

Ensure that your business processes are able to support your promises. Cybercrime risks stifling the development of e-business in the UK. According to a survey by the Confederation of British Industry around two-thirds of organizations experienced a 'serious incident' in 2001, such as hacking, virus attack or credit card fraud. Research also indicates that the larger the business, the more exposed it is to security breaches. Only one-third of companies were confident that their business-to-customer transactions are safe. In addition, a major challenge facing companies in the technology industry is to avoid their products falling into a 'content gap'; that is, the consequences of technology running ahead of the marketing capability to do anything interesting with it. An excellent example of this is the mobile telephone giant Ericsson, which controls 40 per cent of the world's cellular infrastructure. Although Ericsson has some of the most progressive technology in the world, it is struggling to find marketable ideas on what to do with it to drive the sales of its handsets. In the search for content, Ericsson has initiated a programme whereby it gives its technology and office space free to anybody that can come up with a good application for their mobile phones.[74] This is a key area where the creativity of co-members comes to the fore. Innovation should be a three-pronged process. The first prong is the innovative content designers, which means that organizations must focus on attracting and recruiting creative individuals, and giving them the freedom and support to come up with new concepts. The second prong is the consumers who know best what type of content they would like, and the third is a creative communication/PR function which must endeavour to link the two to provide synergy.

A case in point: reed.co.uk

The internet has resulted in barriers to entry being so low that almost anyone with a computer and a modem has the opportunity to attempt to be a cyberspace pioneer. This case study sets out how our site, reed.co.uk, was able to dominate

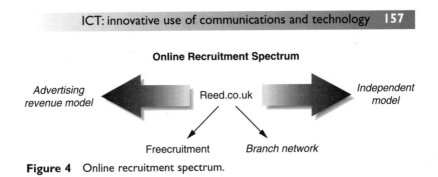

Figure 4 Online recruitment spectrum.

the online recruitment market with a strategy that challenged the business models behind some of its biggest competitors.

Reed.co.uk first came into existence in 1995, making the company the first high-street recruitment agency to gain a presence on the worldwide web. During the early days of the online recruitment market the major players could be placed at the two poles of a broad online recruitment spectrum (Figure 4).

A number of companies such as Stepstone, Monster and Guardian Jobs operated using an advertising revenue model. Such sites targeted recruitment agencies and businesses, offering them the chance to display jobs, for a fee, on their highly advertised and strongly branded sites. Players of this type spent millions of pounds developing their brand; in Stepstone's case this included a £7 million sponsorship deal with Channel 4 Sport.

Typically, advertising revenue sites came to the market in a blaze of publicity. Backed by large media corporations these were sizeable operations that were prepared for, and capable of, taking large losses as they battled to establish their market position.

The independent model applied to specific recruitment agencies. These sites advertised the vacancies placed with them and utilized the strength of their high-street branding and network of consultants. Players of this type included the likes of Michael Page, Hays and Adecco. Originally, reed.co.uk adhered to the independent model and was a relatively small operation.

Our vision was for reed.co.uk to become the leading online marketplace for jobs in the UK. However, by advertising only Reed vacancies, the website was unable to attract the same number of visitors to the site as those with the advertising revenue-based model in the 'general' recruitment market.

The key development in overcoming this obstacle came from an idea submitted through the company's employee suggestion scheme, 'ReedTHINK'. Although the idea could have been deemed to act against Reed's interests, the directors recognized its potential and the co-member who submitted it was awarded a £100 000 bonus.

That idea was 'Freecruitment'. It involved inviting businesses including rival recruitment agencies to advertise as many jobs as they liked on reed.co.uk, for free. The costs of allowing others to use the site are kept relatively low owing to a sophisticated online system that allows Freecruiters to upload jobs onto the site themselves.

The ideology underpinning the Freecruitment approach has its roots deeply entrenched in peoplism. It was the realization that the consumer was becoming more powerful and demanding more for their attention that led reed.co.uk to expand their offering and incorporate the jobs being offered by the competition. While increasing the number of jobs helped to attract potential candidates, Reed Online also took steps to individualize its service to potential candidates by adding industry-specific streams to the site. These streams, which cover a wide range of specialisms from accountancy to zoology (in science specialism – Reed Scientific Personnel), offer additional industry-specific features such as the latest market information, news, advice and updates on the organizations that are recruiting in that sector.

Freecruitment means that the site boasts the largest number of vacancies, by an impressive margin. This brings with it the largest number of site visitors in the online recruitment field. For example, at the end of July 2002, reed.co.uk had over 92 000 jobs advertised. Typically, an advertising revenue model will host in the region of 20 000 jobs, with one example, 'Workthing.co.uk', hosting 18 500 at the time of writing (July 2002). Independent models tend to have slightly fewer jobs, with the Michael Page website offering 15 100 at the time of writing.

The success of Freecruitment was heightened when, in June 2000, the online database that hosts the details of all potential candidates who were applying for jobs on reed.co.uk was made fully compatible with Reed's internal 'Candidates and Clients' database. The streamlined technology allowed consultants to search through the online database for suitable candidates for their own positions and to export the details of these candidates accordingly; in other words, to transfer the candidates' details to the main internal database which handles all of the business and administration processes. As well as allowing manual searching of the database, Reed Online installed a process known as 'autosift', which automatically exports the details of any candidates matching key criteria to their nearest appropriate branch. This ensures that those candidates with sought-after skills are highlighted as quickly as possible. By inviting candidates to register their details if applying to any of the jobs on reed.co.uk, the database grew quickly.

Reed's core revenue relies on getting people into jobs. The fact that reed.co.uk housed the details of thousands of new potential candidates meant that the Reed consultants could tap into a resource that effectively allowed them to target and pluck candidates from the site. Candidates were therefore placed in jobs more quickly, meeting one of our most important business objectives.

Unlike most job boards, on reed.co.uk the candidate also remains in complete control of who sees their CV. Recruiters only gain access if a candidate chooses to apply to their job, and only Reed's own consultants can search the database. This means that individuals will never find themselves in the embarrassing situation where their boss finds out that they are looking for a new job by discovering their details on a recruitment site. Therefore, while reed.co.uk can be classed as a general jobs marketplace it has segmented itself to blowpipe marketing to market today's peoplist job seeker.

Other features have regularly been added to reed.co.uk to enhance the user experience and to target candidates more effectively. Registration on the site also allows access to the 'Job Sleuth' tool, an automated system that emails registrants with new jobs matching their specific search criteria. Although several other recruitment sites also used such a system, Reed were the first to extend this service to short messaging services (SMS): text messages to mobile telephones. Currently, around 300 000 text message job alerts are sent each month, making reed.co.uk users among the best-connected job hunters in the world. A more recent advance has been the 'ANYJOB' function, which allows the individual to apply for and track any job, advertised anywhere in the world, using the information stored at reed.co.uk; a free service allowing candidates to manage their job search from one place.

Through the combination of Freecruitment and Reed's integrated branch network, reed.co.uk has established itself between the poles of the online recruitment spectrum. This was truly innovative unique strategic positioning, which took full advantage of the networked world.

Today, the potential online market remains huge and is still growing; recent survey research conducted by Reed suggests one in three skilled workers look online first for their next job and two out of three human resource directors use the internet for recruitment purposes.

As there are currently more than 500 recruitment internet sites targeting job seekers in the UK, the hefty competition is forcing innovation, with sites enhancing the scope of the services on offer and converging towards the centre of the online recruitment spectrum. Today, the two distinct models have become somewhat blurred as attempts have been made to establish more comprehensive job marketplaces. Recruitment agencies have begun to form strategic alliances with the more traditional advertising-based sites; notably Adecco, which teamed up first with Monster and then acquired JobPilot, and Manpower with GoJobSite. In addition, the advertising-based sites have started to incorporate additional features to their service portfolio in an attempt to differentiate and improve the breadth of their overall offer.

In the future we are likely to see further consolidation in the market and the top players are likely to become stronger. The best alternative for smaller sites is to market themselves to specific audiences; an example is jimfinder.co.uk, which is an engineering recruitment website.

Traffic to reed.co.uk reached record levels in July 2002, with over 1.6 million visits and almost 4.5 million searches conducted. The site again hosted the largest selection of jobs in the UK, as a result of the impact of Freecruitment. The key determinant of this success is an innovative approach to the targeting of candidates through 'clicks and bricks', that is the combination of our website and the branch network.

The thinking is ...

Whether your business is focused on global or domestic expansion, the agility to adapt and accommodate the changing needs and wants of your customers will determine your success. While technology affords marketers the means by which they can collate more data and target customers more effectively, it also empowers customers to self-select on any number of criteria, facilitated by price comparisons and

ethical considerations. In an environment of perpetual instability it is of acute importance that companies have an open,
structured and responsive communication management
strategy, since communication will determine the speed and
accuracy with which companies are able to respond. The use
and misuse of technology is only likely to increase in the
future. This can cause problems that impact not only on business systems, but also on human resource management in
terms of co-member training. Companies must take a holistic
and strategic approach to new technologies, and be aware of
the benefits that technological pioneering can bring.

CHAPTER 8

Concluding thoughts

Peoplism is a paradigm shift, and now there are adjustments to be corrected. It has altered the criteria by which success in the Western world is determined. Many giants of the past are disenfranchised as nimble competitors are better placed to make the most of the new business conditions that prevail. Individualization underpins the movement, causing considerable problems for corporations and governments, both of which are used to setting group-based policies. Business is talent led, real-time and interactive. All markets are competitive and technologically dynamic. Flexibility and agility drive success.

In the Introduction to this book, five challenges were identified as being key to business success in the people economy. This is an appropriate place to revisit them, and summarize the strategic actions and reactions detailed throughout the text.

To refocus human resource management

Companies must support their commitment to co-members by having a peoplist director with strategic responsibilities in the controlling triumvirate. Human resources (HR) departments need to refocus their approach into one of strategic holism, and embrace intuitive intelligence as their benchmark when attracting, recruiting and retaining talent. As ideas and creativity are the currency of success, companies must develop innovative idea deposit schemes and bonuses, with the ultimate goal being to set up a venture peoplist system. At best, companies can only hope to harness particular talent for a limited period.

To realign accounting practice with the key value drivers

The credibility gap in accounting must be filled by changes to accounting practice and an evolution in the mentality of senior managers. The key value drivers in business, co-members, are not considered in accounting practices, nor do they seem to be particularly interested in the reports and analysis produced. Resources dedicated to researching and producing this incomplete information would be better deployed building the company pot by concentrating on the core business goals and focusing on excellent HR management, public relations (PR) and customer service.

Companies should adopt profit:enterprise ratios so that stakeholders are able to discern the levels of innovation and enterprise being driven through the organization. Tighter, more relevant accounts should be produced at shorter time intervals over longer time periods.

To reposition marketing where it is off-target

Companies must have a responsive and responsible attitude to using technology to target consumers, whilst actively losing promiscuous clients and customers.

Developing a corporate badge and garnering excellent public relations is a key business priority, although these must not be pursued at the expense of actually living up to those goals. The process of separating brands from products has clearly accelerated since the early 1990s. Focus on the naked individual, as we will soon witness a complete breakdown in the utility of group distinctions.

To ensure that organizational structures are not stifling success

A triumvirate at the apex provides the flexibility and skills necessary to deliver success. The chief talent officer will rise in importance at the expense of the chief finance officer. Key talent must be given the freedom to transfer across departmental 'silos'. The era of the specialist is fading as the business environment changes too rapidly to indulge knowledge niches, encouraging a concomitant rise in 'enterprising specialists' who are able to have an impact in any part of the company.

To allow corporate culture to evolve

Management communication culture must strive to be as open as possible; it is in corporate interests to make as much information as possible available to customers and co-members to facilitate self-selection.

Companies should create a process culture in which innovation and enterprise behaviours are encouraged, facilitated and rewarded. Small administrative and procedural responses to peoplism, such as the introduction of flexible working, should not be underestimated in their ability to chip away at inflexible corporate culture.

Strive to have a strategy that is unique to your organization. Business strategy is the key intangible asset that will shape all other intangibles, including corporate culture, co-member commitment and your badge. Identify, articulate and develop unique strategic positioning (USP) in both the internal and external functions to this end. USPs must be both flexible and progressive, since the business successes of the future will strategize on the run; confirming intuitive intelligence as the number one sought-after competency for co-members.

Successful long-term strategy is dependent on having joined-up, connected thinking in your company. This is a challenge that stretches beyond checking that all departments are able to recite the corporate motto. With so many personalities and talent pivotal to success, and in a fluid environment where the ability to focus and pay attention through a barrage of information and 'better offers' is a significant challenge to all, systems must be designed to support and facilitate this connectivity.

In addition to the continuing decline of margins and perpetual instability, one trend that will have a huge impact on business over the next decade will be a substantial increase in partnership projects between national and local government agencies and private-sector companies. These result from the impotence of governments to provide services. However, companies should not be seduced by the partnership aspect of these deals, since government is an unreliable bedfellow.

Peoplism is stripping individuals of long-held securities. Sense of community has dwindled. Money can no longer buy success; bad ideas will fail no matter how extravagant the backing. The protections of family and religion grow ever weaker. And it is at precisely this time that restrictions on governmental activity prevent states from addressing such vulnerabilities. Traditional securities for old age are being drawn back, and governments are discovering that they are incapable of helping those who are feeling the strongest chill of peoplism; those without the nous to navigate the peoplist market. Trade unions will provide assistance in the short term, as their collective standing is solidified in response to the mushrooming market differentials for those with talent and those without.

The state has broken down. Individuals are disrobed. Disconnected thinking and dysfunctionality persist within organizations at all levels. The challenges to cope are immense and, as a business leader, the daunting future keeps me awake at night.

CHAPTER 9

The daunting future

Not to be read alone at night – the future is frightening.

The status quo has served us well, but the future will serve us ill. Peoplism is no kinder than capitalism, a fact that will be compounded as the trends identified throughout this book build in strength and clash with one another, causing friction and dysfunction in society. The capabilities and responsibilities of governments and business will be unrecognizable in the future. There is significant cause for concern. Nations are competing to move up the food chain. As a result of the erosion of state power, the overlap between the public and private sectors as service providers will become a permanent feature of society. The symptoms of peoplism, diminishing margins and perpetual instability, will condense and cause havoc for governments, individuals and businesses. The future for citizens, co-members, investors, parents and children is daunting. For all but the very few, it will bring the worst of times.

Future societies

In the future, citizens in the Western world will not only have to carry an identity card, but part of those cards will form a charge card to each individual's 'citizen's account'. This is the solution necessary to promote an increased choice of welfare services while requiring more responsibility from individuals. It is grounded in the fundamental that those who can pay do pay, and those who cannot, do not. Each adult will hold an account card like a credit card, which can be swiped when a state-funded service has been used. The account will be debited when an individual utilizes a state service, such as jobseeker's allowance, and credited when an individual contributes to their account when in work by way of a sur-tax. The longer an individual uses any state benefits or services, the longer the period they will have to pay a percentage of their income over and above income tax to balance their account. Should death arrive before the balance is in equilibrium, the account will be reconciled against their estate.

As now, everybody will be entitled to state schooling for free, and to further education, the cost of which will be debited to their account. No repayments will be required until an individual has reached the level of earnings where they are required to pay income tax. All state services used after the age of 18 will be treated in the same way. Prisoners will assist in paying off the massive costs of their detention through employment upon release, not in an arbitrary manner that would discourage rehabilitation, but by affordable means. No longer will the Nicholas van Hoogstratens, Jonathan Aitkens and Jeffrey Archers of this world reside in Her Majesty's Prisons at great cost to the taxpayer, only to be released into luxurious wealth. With a citizen's account, they will have to repay the state for the costs incurred during their custody. For the actor or freelance programmer who receives generous wages when in work, but presently claims jobseeker's allowance for the 4 or 5 months in between contracts, the citizen's account gives a fairer representation of when assistance is genuinely needed, and when it is not. As employment becomes increasingly fractious for many portfolio workers this provision is an important one. The citizen's account will also mean a higher standard of service as the provider will be unaware of who is paying for the service and who is not, and will therefore have to treat everyone with equally high standards of customer service.

The future is frightening for law and order

It is clear that the British prison system is not working, a pattern being replicated across Europe. The UK is already 7000 prisoners over capacity and has experienced riots, unrest and protests as a result.

In the near future there will be an urgent need for increased flexibility in prison reform. We are beginning to have an international outlook in respect to health provision, and global solutions for our prison dilemma will also be considered. While care will have to be taken to avoid any appearance of imperialist arrogance, some of those residing at Her Majesty's pleasure will be outsourced to secure, and comfortable, prisons in a country where the expenditure per prisoner is a fraction of the £34 524 a year in capital and current costs each new prisoner costs in the UK.

Such a programme will benefit all parties, not least the prisoner, who will see a reduction in their sentence for serving it overseas, and/or a gratuity upon release to facilitate their rehabilitation. The savings made from that individual serving their term overseas will fund this. Importantly, there could also be increased investment into training and education as a result of reduced accommodation costs. Prisoners who remain in the UK for other reasons will benefit from less crowded establishments. The host country – one possibility is Tanzania, which has a good human rights record and solid relationship with the UK – would make a profit from housing the prisoners. The taxpayer will have lower prison costs to support and reoffending rates will be reduced through the increased investment in training. There are testing times ahead for the Home Office, and this radical action, and reconnected thinking, will be necessary to prevent the nation's very own prison drama becoming a crisis.

A disastrous outlook for education

There has been a failure by successive governments to pay some teachers their worth, and as a result union power is strong. Now it is very difficult for schools to ask for any added value from a highly unionized workforce. Finding good teachers is extremely difficult, to say the least. The government let pupils down badly when it agreed to pressure from the unions for a standard salary applicable to teachers of all subjects across all parts of the country. When an average salary is set, everyone who is likely to earn below that sum finds it appealing, while those with above-average market value, such as teachers with a skill in maths, science or information technology, are persuaded to leave, or dissuaded from joining, the profession. Salaries must reflect market values, not central rules. It is ridiculous that a primary teacher in a small rural school can earn the same salary as a teacher at an inner-city comprehensive struggling to motivate moody adolescents through their GCSEs.

The central theme of the peoplist economy is that the most important driver of value creation is the enterprise and creativity of individuals. Unless the government puts enterprise at the heart of the curriculum, and develops examinations in the subject, it will increasingly fall to companies belatedly to develop the raw material entering the workforce with the skills required. Enterprise education is just the tip of the iceberg of what is needed. A complete re-focus is required by companies, educators and policiticans. We must all learn a new game.

One way to drive forward education is to teach teaching in the classrooms. As we move through the era of lifelong learning, everybody will at some stage have to utilize teaching skills, whether in the classroom, as a coach in the workplace, or as a parent. Teaching is a vocational subject that has applicability to the students. Not only will such a development promote the profession and provide assistance in the classroom, it bestows a vital skill that is increasingly important in the workplace.

Trouble ahead for government

Companies are increasingly discerning over their choice of suppliers and contractors. As the government is unable to provide most services in the people economy, it must rely on private support-service contractors to do so in public–private partnership agreements. While there is over £100 billion of public funds committed to future private finance initiatives

(PFIs), the government is damaging itself by being a promiscuous purveyor of PFI. Successful private-sector operators will not tender for the small margins, not to mention the uncertainty and bureaucracy that are on offer in such projects. Those who have done so are unlikely to do so a second time, given the trouble that so many companies have had with partnership in the past. The first private operator in a field takes all the risk and blazes the trail, but if that operator is rejected in a storm of negative publicity they are unlikely to bid again. High-profile public-sector contracts bring high-profile risks. Shares in Nestor Healthcare fell by an amazing 41 per cent in 2 days after the group announced the loss of a key government contract in July 2002. A similar loss of investment appeal has befallen Capita, Securicor, Atkins and Jarvis, all of whom are high-profile government contractors.

Thus, not only will the ability of government to provide services be reduced, but its ability to team up with good private-sector operatives will also deteriorate.

The future of famine

It is daunting that social divisions look set to continue and widen in the future. These massive disparities of income cause misery for those at the bottom end of the scale, which can channel the anger of millions towards the Western world. Three billion citizens, representing over 45 per cent of the world's population, are living on less than US$2 per day. Over one-fifth of the world's population, 1.2 billion people, are living on less than US$1 a day, while billions more live in squalor and desperation, generation after generation.

It is clear that the preconditions of hostility are firmly entrenched across continents. Domestic governments around the world have long heeded the lessons of past revolutions: that all sections of the population must be sustained at a basic level of income to minimize the ever-present risk of revolt; hence the complex welfare systems in place in all developed countries. In our global village, the resentment towards opulence and excess wealth, which the West has come to represent, is no less dangerous than the resentment towards the landowners from the working classes centuries ago. Yet the *means* of revolt, as we witnessed with such horror and helplessness on 11 September 2001, have changed vastly.

Governments will be forced to act by introducing a world tax to draw a measured and proportionate contribution from all donor states. Such contributions will not be akin to gesture donations or aid, but a constant levy of an amount that will make life-changing differences in the developing world.

The World Bank estimated in 1997 that the cost of eradicating the worst forms of poverty is US$225 billion per annum. Although daunting, such a sum is attainable when compared with the riches of Western countries. By taxing 1 per cent of the gross domestic product (GDP) of the richest 25 countries, on a GDP per capita basis, over US$310 billion would be raised. The tax would be levied on a sliding scale from the most wealthy of the top 25 countries, which would pay 1.5 per cent of GDP, to the least wealthy of the top 25 paying 0.5 per cent of GDP. In reducing the tax rate and increasing the tax coverage to all countries with GDP per capita above the world's average, the contribution would be shared among all of the richest nations. The International Monetary Fund, which has in place the infrastructure for distributing loans to developing countries, might be the administrator-in-chief of the tax revenue, and auditor as to the money's appropriate use.

The project is enormously ambitious. In an age of global terrorism, it is also connected thinking. By demonstrating a commitment to raising the quality of life where such an improvement is desperately needed, not merely where it is politically acceptable to do so, the West will dilute the hostility that may otherwise fuel future terrorist attacks. A world tax will echo the political mantra of our domestic security in the UK; to be tough on crime and tough on the causes of crime. In so doing, it is a small price to pay.

Future demographics

The current rate of resource depletion is unsustainable. Over one-third of the world's natural resources have been consumed in the past 40 years. We may be faced with a situation in 50 years in which innovation and technological change can no longer facilitate lifestyle enhancement to the same degree that we have enjoyed. We may be faced with a downsizing of our lifestyles, and companies that have assumed ever-increasing levels of prosperity and its companion, consumer consumption, will have to adjust strategically to this. With two-thirds of adults aged over 45 in the UK already overweight, and one in five adults clinically obese, we will see in the long-term future a drive to breed smaller people, both in height and in weight, as they take up fewer resources. In the people economy we no longer need just farmers and fighters, but brains, and there will be scientific research and an element of genetic streaming to this end.

The key skills required for success in the people economy cannot be passed down from generation to generation in the same way that capital was. Family businesses will therefore cease to be. The inherent logic of the peoplist economy is for downward as well as upward mobility; simply put, education must facilitate the progression of an individual into becoming a contributor to the peoplist economy, regardless of the success of his or her immediate family.

Traditional relationships will be reconfigured so that they combine a dynamic and a support partner. There will be no standard gender demarcations, although because the economy is moving from old men to young women we can expect to see an increasing number of males playing the support role to their high-flying partners.

Those who succeeded in the capitalist economy – the huge conglomerates and multinationals – made so much money that seemingly generous donations to charity and the setting up of trust funds were very small change indeed. In peoplist times, margins are too tight for such indulgences. Competition is quick and merciless, and surplus profits will be neither achievable, nor tolerable to stakeholders such as consumers and suppliers. The winners will be talented individuals; they will make the money, and they will spend it. The actions of a few altruistic souls aside, charitable donations of major significance will cease to be.

Future finance

The FTSE 100 Index in 2030

Increasingly, listings such as the FTSE 100, the list of the UK's 100 leading shares by valuation, tell us nothing. Of the high-technology companies that broke into the FTSE 100 during the late 1990s only the software group Sage remains there today. Investors have been misled that high capitalization is an indication of either permanence or profitability.

Equity/financial markets

Shareholder value of companies is an inappropriate guide to management performance. Increasingly, this fact is highlighted by volatile equity valuations, the repercussions of which have been witnessed both as the dotcom boom came to an inauspicious end, and in the recent and disturbing accounting scandals in the USA. The separation of company valuation from actual company financial performance has come back to haunt the financial markets.

In 1990 two of the stocks that would have been essential in any investor's portfolio were ICI and Marks & Spencer. Amazingly, shares in the two are actually lower now, in real terms, than they were in 1990. Even the most cautious of investors will be caught out in unpredictable markets.

Equities, like gold, are becoming an artificial currency, buoyed not by their value, but by market demand. Markets have been overvalued since the 1990s, if not for longer. There remains the fundamental problem of how to value

Table 1

Average P/E ratio across FTSE 100	FTSE Valuation	Total mark cap across FTSE 100 (£bn)	Loss (£bn)
Current ratio 19	3914	969.49	
18	3708	918.46·	51.03
17	3502	867.43	102.06
16	3296	816.40	153.09
15	3090	765.38	204.12
14	2884	714.35	255.15
13	2678	663.33	306.18
12	2472	612.30	357.21
11	2266	561.28	408.24

This table was accurate as of 25 July 2002.

public companies reasonably. At the time of writing, the FTSE is valued at a price/earnings (P/E) ratio of approximately 19 across the board, a figure somewhat higher than the range of 10–13, which is the traditional conservative benchmark. Table 1 indicates the value of the FTSE should earnings remain the same but FTSE equity be traded in line with lower P/E multiples. It remains to be seen what the reaction would be, should we witness a drop in the FTSE to the levels indicated in our benchmark. In the people economy, it may be more realistic to have an even lower P/E, which would have an enormous impact on the investment community.

Building a peoplist investment strategy

The field of investment will also alter significantly as stocks and shares become increasingly risky. The most prudent investment strategy involves selling shares, which are an unreliable investment, and returning to basics by buying agricultural land. Agricultural investment is more prudent than other forms of property because it requires very little maintenance, and in most cases will be maintained for free by the sitting tenant. It is also possible to buy and sell agricultural land without paying capital gains tax, enjoying a roll-over release, and it is more favourably treated by inheritance tax. As the government presses on in its policy of building thousands of new houses, it will loosen planning permission on agricultural land, taking the pressure off the stewardship of the land. Thus, the premium on agricultural land will only increase.

In the future, we will pay people to protect our capital. Capital maintenance, not capital growth, will become the order of the day, although this will not necessarily be easy to achieve.

Pensions

The number of pensioners in the UK will overtake the number of children by 2007, and exceed it by nearly two million by 2025. This ageing British population will be competing against younger populations in the USA, southeast Asia and elsewhere, to serious economic consequence. According to AXA, one of the UK's biggest insurers, the UK faces at least a £27 billion pensions shortfall at present, which makes the future even more daunting, as this shortfall will only be compounded in the future. The strain for companies is apparent, and final salary schemes are being closed apace.

Six of every ten are now closed to new members. The implications for companies are staggering. At the time of writing, the market capitalization of British Airways is less than £2 billion; however, its company pension funds are in excess of £15 billion. Steelmaker Corus has a pension fund of £9.1 billion, worth five times its market value of £1.8 billion. Companies will continue to be burdened by the constant liabilities upon them.

Public confidence in pensions has been eroded, hammered down by an increasingly complex system, plunging stock markets and the attractions of investing in property. Thus, the problem is further exacerbated as many of the younger generation consciously turn their backs on a system that is in danger of spiralling out of control. The summary of investments over the past 15 years reveals an interesting trend. In 1986, 45 per cent of all pension fund investments were placed in UK equities, 14 per cent in overseas equities and 12 per cent in UK property. At the beginning of 2000 an average of 52 per cent was invested in UK equities, 21 per cent in overseas equities and less than 5 per cent in UK property. Thus we have witnessed a marked increase in the value of pensions being invested in the risky world of equities. The cost of annuities is crippling pensions and tax advantages have been withdrawn.

Another factor of the pension problem is that we are living longer. In 1950 a man reaching the pensionable age of 65 could expect to live for a further 11.7 years; today expectations have increased to 15.87. While at present there are more than three people of working age funding each pension, in 2036 the Institute of Actuaries warns that this will reduce to 2.4. Past governments have taken a huge risk by relying on the income from current financing to fund its obligations to pensioners, but as there are fewer wage earners per pensioner now, and with the increasing transience and choices facing those of working age, this funding is far from secure.

Future plc

Businesses are tied up. In the future companies will increasingly share talent simultaneously, and the key question will be who best to share with, although it is not certain that companies will be in a position to pick and choose. Individuals will retain ultimate sovereignty over their time in this world of work, and we may soon see the scenario where companies in a competitive market are forced to share a worker simultaneously with a rival, perhaps even one that is trying to solve the same problem or generate the same idea. This can already be seen in areas such as information technology contractors, but will increasingly apply to a wider remit of specialisms in the future, including generic 'enterprising workers'. The traditional view of the career as consisting purely of paid employment will disappear. Instead, expect employment to form one part of a more varied career which merges with other activities to become more a series of life experiences. Charitable work, family-centred work and career breaks will be the norm.

The opportunity to experience different industries, careers and indeed activities through different experiences will generally increase the cross-fertilization of ideas and best practice across industries. For instance, although an increasing trend, only a tiny majority of private-sector companies specifically seek to recruit employees from the charitable/ voluntary sector or to identify areas of best practice in that sector that might be applicable to their businesses. The same problem is more acute on the part of charities, some of whom still need to learn from the private sector how to run the business side of their operations. Tomorrow's people will bring with them work experience from a variety of commercial and not-for-profit environments, increasing awareness and understanding between the two sectors to the benefit of both. Public limited companies will increasingly deploy the talents of individuals who are involved in the not-for-profit sector, since they have the key experience of running successful operations with very tight resources, often needing to motivate volunteers. Businesses will have to learn from them the skills of leading and motivating people as margins evaporate.

The thinking is ...

Be alarmed: not only is the government unable to provide many of the services it delivered in the past, its ability to partner with dynamic private-sector companies will be severely restricted in the future, leaving the job to second-rate providers. *Be overawed* by the rapidity with which the pool of global resources is reducing; and be prepared for the time when the breeding of smaller, more resource-friendly people, will be subsidized by nation-states. *Be unnerved* that in the future your company will be forced to share its talent with other companies, possibly even with direct competitors. *Be discouraged* that despite the increasing premium on human talent as the key value driver in the people economy, there is still a ghettoization of education. *Be disheartened* that with the enormity of changes taking place, the world will work in more of a Darwinian 'survival of the fittest' principle than ever before. Those who would rely on the state, on their family or on charities are most at risk. The future is daunting.

Glossary

Badge (*n.*) – a brand that spans multiple products and services, promoted by emphasizing distinctive elements of the supplier rather than the individual products

Co-member (*n.*) – the term used within Reed to represent everyone who works for the company as an internal client, rather than an 'employee'

Disconnected thinking (*n.*) – when business purpose, action and outcomes are misaligned, caused by poor management, short-termism, misdirected reward strategies, etc.

Enterprise learning (*n.*) – the process of improving enterprise skills. This can be done partly through practising the generation of ideas and demonstrating the value of innovation

Enterprise skills (*n.*) – more useful in the peoplist economy than traditional qualifications, enterprise skills include creativity, innovation, communication, motivation, the ability to problem solve and the ability to create unusual opportunities

Idea-lization (*n.*) – The process by which creativity is brought about

Intuitive intelligence (*n.*) – the ability to think rapidly and decisively without relying on traditional methods of logic, demonstrating a preference for the unknown and unconventional, while having a high level of confidence in one's own ideas

Peoplism (*n.*) – an economic state where individuals own and control the most important factors of production: their human ability

Peoplist (*adj.*) – demonstrating characteristics associated with peoplism

Notes

1 Winston Fletcher, *The Guardian*, 2 Jan. 2001.

2 Gabby Hinsliff, *The Observer*, 3 Feb. 2002.

3 Jill Sherman, *The Times*, 29 Jan. 2002.

4 Norota Nosowicz, *The Observer*, 4 Feb. 2002.

5 Simon Goodley, *The Telegraph*, 7 Feb. 2002.

6 Anon., *The Daily Express*, 26 Feb. 2002.

7 Anon., *The Telegraph*, 6 Dec. 2001.

8 UN Human Development Report, as reported in *The New York Times*, 9 Sept. 1998.

9 Phillip Brown and Hugh Lauder, *The Guardian*, 29 Oct. 2001.

10 Simon Briscoe, *The Financial Times*, 14 Aug. 2002.

11 Christopher Adams and Nicholas Timmins, *The Financial Times*, 3 Dec. 2001.

12 Richard Tomkins, *The Financial Times*, 12 Feb. 2002.

13 British Crime Survey, *IPPR*, 31 Oct. 2001.

14 Nicholas Timmins, *The Financial Times*, 22 Aug. 2001.

15 Jill Treanor, *The Guardian*, 10 June 2000.

16 Johann Hari, *The New Statesman*, 3 Dec. 2002.

17 Steve Doughty, *The Daily Mail*, 31 Jan. 2002.

18 Claire Wallerstein, *The Guardian*, 21 Feb. 2002.

19 Jill Sherman, *The Times*, 29 Jan. 2002.

20 Catherine Morrison, *The Guardian*, 28 Jan. 2002.

21 Anon., *The Metro*, 19 Dec. 2001.

22 Ahal Besorai, *e.business.uk*, Jan. 2002.

23 Tony Soffe, *e.business*, Jan. 2002.

24 Des Dearlove, *The Times*, 25 Apr. 2002.

25 Juan Enriquez, *As the Future Catches You*, Crown Business, 2001.

26 Lee Hecht Harrison, 'Beyond downsizing: staffing and workforce management for the millennium' (available at www.lhh.com).

27 Meg Carter, *The Financial Times*, 26 Apr. 2002.

28 Phil Dourado, *The Business*, 24/25 Mar. 2002.

29 Lorna Duckworth, *The Independent*, 29 Oct. 2001.

30 Alison Maitland, *The Financial Times*, 20 Sept. 2001.

31 Pam Belluck, *The New York Times*, 4 Dec. 2000.

32 Anon., *Personnel Today*, 6 Nov. 2001.

33 David Turner, *The Financial Times*, June 2002.

34 Nicole Martin, *The Telegraph*, 6 Mar. 2002.

35 Lina Saigol, *The Financial Times*, 14 Aug. 2001.

36 Anon., *The Economist*, 25 Aug. 2001.

37 Will Woodward, *The Guardian*, 20 May 2002.

38 Nigel Morris, *The Independent*, 29 Nov. 2001.

39 Anna Stewart, *Business*, 12/13 May 2002.

40 Robert Kovach, *The Financial Times*, 30 Aug. 2001.

41 Alison Maitland, *The Financial Times*, 21 Sept. 2001.

42 Robert Kovach, *Business*, circa Mar. 2002.

43 Robert Taylor, 'Britain's world of work – myths and realities', *ESRC Future of Work Programme Seminar Series*.

44 David Summer Smith, *Marketing Business*, Oct. 2001.

45 Michael Skapinker and Alison Maitland, *The Financial Times*, 6 Mar. 2002.

46 Anon., *The Financial Times*, 31 Oct. 2001.

47 Russell Hotten, *The Times*, 29 Apr. 2002.

48 Anon., 'Week in numbers', *The Observer*, 7 Apr. 2002.

49 Terry Macalister, *The Guardian*, 14 May 2002.

50 Frank Kane, *The Observer*, 20 May 2002.

51 Sophie Barker, *The Telegraph*, 20 May 2002 .

52 Reed Accountancy Personnel survey, *Accountancy Age Magazine*, 20 Sept. 2001.

53 Simon Targett, *The Financial Times Fund Management Supplement*, 20 May 2002.

54 Lee Hecht Harrison, *Downsizing Report*, 2001, p. 16.

55 Simon Caulkin, *The Change Agenda*, Report for the Chartered Institute of Personnel and Development, p. 4.

56 Vernon Ellis, Accenture survey, *The Times*, 22 Aug. 2001.

57 Best Practice Report No. 88 on Managing Innovation, The Industrial Society, Jan. 2002.

58 Virginia Matthews, *The Business*, 2/5 June 2002.

59 Richard Reeves, *The Guardian*, 11 June 2002.

60 Alexander Garrett, *The Observer*, 19 Aug. 2001.

61 Stephen Overell, *The Financial Times*, 27 May 2002.

62 Jane Pickard, *People Management*, 19 Apr. 2001.

63 See Charles Leadbetter, '*New Measures for the New Economy*', Report for the OECD, May 1999.

64 Anon., Business outlook, *The Independent*, 23 Jan. 2002.

65 Deborah Doane and Alex MacGillivray, *Economic Sustainability: The Business of Staying in Business*, New Economics Foundation, London, Mar. 2001.

66 Ernst & Young, *Measures That Matter*, 1997.

67 David Skryme, 'Measuring the value of knowledge', *Business Intelligence*, London, 1999.

68 PricewaterhouseCoopers, 'Value reporting', *Forecast*, 2000.

69 Tony Pilch, '*Dynamic Reporting for a Dynamic Economy*', The Smith Institute/Academy of Enterprise, Oct. 2000.

70 John Cassy, Survey conducted by Hill and Knowlton, *The Guardian*, 29 Apr. 2002.

71 Virgina Matthews, *The Financial Times*, 30 Jan 2002.
72 Robert Bailhache, *'Business'* 12/13 May 2002.
73 Simon Caulkin, *The Observer*, 7 Apr. 2002.
74 Zad Rogers, *The Guardian*, 7 Feb. 2000.

Index